▶Select Readings

Upper-Intermediate

Jean Bern

Linda Le

OXFORD

UNIVERSITY PRESS

OXFORD
UNIVERSITY PRESS

198 Madison Avenue, New York, NY 10016 USA
Great Clarendon Street, Oxford OX2 6DP England

Oxford New York
Auckland Bangkok Buenos Aires Cape Town
Chennai Dar es Salaam Delhi Hong Kong
Istanbul Karachi Kolkata Kuala Lumpur
Madrid Melbourne Mexico City Mumbai
Nairobi São Paulo Shanghai Taipei
Tokyo Toronto

OXFORD is a trademark of Oxford University Press.

ISBN 0-19-438601-5

**Library of Congress Cataloging-in-Publication
Data**

Bernard, Jean 1944–
    Select readings: upper-intermediate / by Jean
Bernard and Linda Lee.
        p. cm.
    ISBN 0-19-438601-5
    1. English language—Textbooks for foreign
speakers.
    2. Readers. I. Lee, Linda. II. Title.

PE1128.B5344 2003
428.6'4—dc22   2003–056534

Editorial Manager: Nancy Leonhardt
Senior Editor: Chris Balderston
Editor: Patricia O'Neill
Associate Editor: Nishka Chandrasoma
Art Director: Lynn Luchetti
Art Editor: Justine Eun
Production Manager: Shanta Persaud
Production Controller: Eve Wong
Cover design: Tom Hawley, Hawley Design
Cover photo: Andre Jenny/Alamy

Printing (last digit): 10 9 8 7 6 5 4 3 2

Printed in Hong Kong.

ACKNOWLEDGMENTS

Realia by: Aaron Hershman (pp. 94, 97, and 108),
Elizabeth Onorato (pp. 13, 24, 35, 47, 61, 73, 85, 98,
112, 124, 136, and 149)

Maps: Map Resource–Vector Atlas Collection/
Modified by Aaron Hershman (pp. 169–173)

***The publishers would like to thank the
following for their permission to reproduce
photographs:*** © 2003 Estate of Pablo Picasso/
Artists Rights Society (ARS)/New York Réunion des
Musées Nationaux/Art Resource, NY: 2; From "A
Whack on the Side of the Head" by Roger von Oech/
Warner Books: 3; Alamy: John Foxx, 14; Clive Offley/
www.newint.org: 15; Chris Buck: 25, 26;
Popperphoto/Retrofile.com: 36; Reuters: Jim Bourg,
37; ElektraVision/Indexstock: 48; CartoonBank: Leo
Cullum, 49; Kjeld Duits: 62; Fred Weir: 74; Pictures
Colour Library/Alamy: 75; Kwame Zikomo/
SuperStock: 86; Justine Eun/OUP: 87; Photo
Illustration by Rebecca Swiller, Photo by Robert
Harbison/Christian Science Monitor: 99; The
Pierpont Morgan Library/Art Resource, NY: 100;
Indexstock: David Ball, 113; Photodisc/Picturequest:
Scott T. Baxter, 114; Brand X Pictures/Alamy: 125;
Archivo Iconographic, S.A./ CORBIS: 126; CORBIS:
Roger Ressmeyer, 137; First Light/ImageState: 138

***The publishers would like to thank the
following for their permission to reproduce
text:***

p. 4 From *A Whack on the Side of the Head* by Roger
von Oech. Copyright © 1983, 1990 by Roger von Oech.
By permission of Warner Books, Inc.
15   From *New Internationalist*, May 1992. Used by
permission
26   From *Life*, © 1998 TIME Inc. Reprinted by
permission.
37   From *The International Herald Tribune*, July 3,
2002. Reprinted by permission.
49   Reprinted with the permission of *Human
Resources Magazine* (November 2001). Published by
the Society for Human Resource Management,
Alexandria, VA.
63   This article first appeared in *Think Magazine*,
June 1961. Used by permission.
75   This article first appeared in *The Christian
Science Monitor*, Copyright © Fred Weir. Used by
permission of the author.
87   Copyright © 2002, *The Chronicle of Higher
Education*. Reprinted with permission.
101 This article first appeared in *The Christian
Science Monitor* on July 12, 2002, and is reproduced
with permission. Copyright © 2002 The Christian
Science Monitor (www.csmonitor.com). All rights
reserved.
114 Copyright © 1999 *U.S. News & World Report*,
L.P. Reprinted with permission.
126 From *The Importance of Understanding*.
Copyright © Ayer Company Publishers. Used by
permission.
138 From *Sharing the Universe: Perspectives on
Extraterrestrial Life*, published by Berkeley Hills
Books. Used by permission.

▶ Acknowledgments

The publisher would like to thank the following teachers whose comments, reviews and assistance were instrumental in the development of *Select Readings:*

Ann Mei-Yu Chang
Ann-Marie Hadzima
Beatrice Hsiao-Tsui Yang
Brett Reynolds
Chia-Yi Sun
Chi-Fan Lin
Ching-Kang Liu
Christine Chen-Ju Chen
Christopher E. Cuadro
Chuan-Ta Chao
Colin Gullberg
David W.Y. Dai
Douglas I-Ping Ho
Ellen Margaret Head
Florence Yi-Hui Chiou
Frances J. Shiobara
Fujiko Sano
Greg Stinnett

Hideaki Narita
Hsiu-Chieh Chen
Hyun-Woo Lee
Jessica Hsin-Hwa Chen
Jong-Bok Kim
Jong-Yurl Yoon
Joyce Yu-Hua Lee
Kabyong Park
Kazuko Unosawa
Kun-liang Chuang
Kyungbin Yi
Maggie Sokolik
Makoto Shimizu
Maureen Chiu-Yu Tseng
Meredith Pike-Baky
Maosung Lin
Monica Li-Feng Kuo
Patricia Pei-Chun Che

Paul Cameron
Pei-Yin Lu
Peng-Hsiang Chen
Richard Solomons
Robin Cheng-Hsing Tsai
Russell Lefko
Sherry Hsin-Ying Li
Stella Wen-Hui Li
Stephen Mendenhall
Stephen Slater
Steven Donald
Susan Shu-Hua Chou
Tsuh-Lai Huang
Won Park
Ying-Chien Chang
Yu-Chen Hsu

The authors would like to thank the following OUP staff for their support and assistance in the development of *Select Readings:*

Chris Balderston
Julia Chang
Vickie Chang
Tina Chen
JJ Lee

Jason Lee
Chang Oh Lim
Hannah Lee
Constance Mo
Paul Riley

Sumio Takiguchi
Cherry Wu
Ted Yoshioka

► Contents

►Scope and Sequence

	Content	Reading Skill	Building Vocabulary	Language Focus
Chapter 1 What Is Creative Thinking?	Suggestions for learning to think creatively	Identifying main ideas	Figures of speech	Noun clauses
Chapter 2 Why I Quit the Company	Explanation of an employee's decision to resign	Distinguishing fact from opinion	Phrasal verbs	Past conditional sentences
Chapter 3 The Body Shop	Using tissue engineering to repair the human body	Inferencing	Using context to guess meaning	Modals of possibility
Chapter 4 And the Big Winners Were…	Impact of World Cup soccer on players, fans, and host countries	Supporting main ideas	Using prefixes to determine meaning	Direct quotations
Chapter 5 Listen Up	Becoming an effective listener	Recognizing sentence transitions	Using adverbs and intensifiers	Using punctuation: dashes, colons, and semicolons
Chapter 6 Don't Let Stereotypes Warp Your Judgment	Harmful effects of stereotyping	Recognizing sources	Using verbs as adjectives	Using relative clauses with *who, which,* or *that*

►Scope and Sequence

	Content	Reading Skill	Building Vocabulary	Language Focus
Chapter 7 East Meets West on Love's Risky Cyberhighway	Finding a partner via the Internet	Recognizing diverse points of view	Using modifiers	*It's (not) +* verb + *-ing*
Chapter 8 Students Won't Give Up Their French Fries	American students' obsession with food	Scanning for specific information	Idiomatic expressions	Reported speech
Chapter 9 Getting Into the Game	Appreciating the social and educational value of electronic games	Following a story line	Compound words	Gerunds as complements
Chapter 10 Call of the Riled	Cell phone etiquette	Recognizing paragraph transitions	Synonyms and antonyms; using suffixes *-ful* and *-less*	Reduced relative clauses
Chapter 11 The Art of Reading	Suggestions for becoming a skillful reader	Recognizing analogies	Word forms	Expressing similarity and difference
Chapter 12 When E.T. Calls	Exploring the possibility of extraterrestrial life	Recognizing scenarios	Nouns derived from adjectives	Future perfect

▶ Introduction

To the Teacher

Select Readings is a series of reading texts for pre-intermediate through upper-intermediate students of English. In all the levels, high-interest reading passages serve as springboards for reading skills development, vocabulary building, language analysis, and thought-provoking discussions and writing.

In **Select Readings–Upper-Intermediate,** the readings represent a wide range of genres (newspaper and magazine articles, essays, and book excerpts) gathered from well-respected sources such as the *International Herald Tribune, U.S. News & World Report*, and *Life* magazine.

Components

The complete **Select Readings–Upper-Intermediate** program includes the following components:

- *Student Book*

- *Quizzes and Answer Key.* This is available for downloading at *www.oup.com/elt/teacher/selectreadings*. This easy-to-use instructor's companion includes an answer key for all activities in the Student Book and a reproducible, one-page quiz for each chapter.

- *Cassettes/CDs.* Two accompanying audio cassettes or CDs feature recordings of all of the reading passages in the book.

General Approach to Reading Instruction

The following principles have guided our approach throughout the development of **Select Readings:**

- **Exposing students to a variety of text types and genres helps them develop more effective reading skills.** Students learn to handle the richness and depth of writing styles they will encounter as they read more widely in English.

- **Readers become engaged with a selection when they are asked to respond personally to its theme.** While comprehension questions help students see if they have understood the information in a reading, discussion questions ask students to consider the issues raised by the passage.

- **Readers sharpen their reading, vocabulary-building, and language analysis skills when skills work is tied directly to the content and language of each reading passage.** This book introduces students to reading skills such as skimming and scanning, vocabulary-building strategies such as finding synonyms and using phrasal verbs, and language study topics such as reduced clauses.

- **Good readers make good writers.** Reading helps students develop writing skills, while writing experience helps students become better readers.

- **Background knowledge plays an important role in reading comprehension.** An important goal of *Select Readings* is to illustrate how thinking in advance about the topic of a reading prepares readers to better comprehend and interact with a text.

Chapter Overview

Each chapter in *Select Readings* includes the eight sections described below. Suggested time frames for covering the material are also given.

1. Opening Page (5 to 15 minutes)

The purpose of this page is to draw readers into the theme and content of the chapter.

Teaching Suggestions:

- Call students' attention to the *Chapter Focus* box. Give them a chance to think about the content and skills they are about to study and to set their own learning goals for the chapter.

- Ask students to identify what they see in the photo or artwork on the page and guess what the chapter is about. Have them read the quotation, restate it in their own words, and then say if they agree with it. Finally, ask what connection there might be between the image and the quotation.

2. Before You Read (30 to 40 minutes)

One question in each *Before You Read* section asks students to reflect on their prior knowledge of the chapter's topic. Giving students time to think about and discuss this question is an essential part of helping them activate their background knowledge on the topic. A second activity in the *Before You Read* section invites students to practice pre-reading skills such as skimming and scanning. Effective readers use these pre-reading skills regularly to get an initial feel for the content and organization of the reading passage.

Teaching Suggestions:

- Make sure that students understand the purpose of the *Before You Read* activities. Explain that activating prior knowledge will help them to better comprehend the reading passage.

- Encourage student participation in the activities by having people work in small groups to complete the activities.

- React to the content of students' ideas rather than to the grammatical accuracy of their responses.

3. Reading Passage (60 to 75 minutes)

In general, the readings become increasingly longer and more complex as the chapters progress. To help students successfully tackle each passage we have provided the following support tools:

Vocabulary glosses. Challenging words and expressions are glossed throughout the readings. In most cases, we have glossed chunks of words (e.g., *launch a campaign*) instead of individual vocabulary items (e.g., *launch*). This approach helps students develop a better sense of how important context is to understanding the meaning of new words.

Culture and Language Notes. On pages 150–168, students will find explanations for cultural references and language usage that appear in blue type in the readings. Notes are provided on a wide range of topics from scientific information such as NASA, to geographical references such as the former U.S.S.R., to famous people such as Lewis Carroll.

Numbered lines. For easy reference, every fifth line of each reading passage is numbered.

Recorded reading passages. Listening to someone reading a text aloud helps language learners see how words are grouped in meaningful chunks, thus aiding comprehension.

At the end of each reading, there is a short section giving biographical information on the author or information about the source. This information helps students develop a richer context for the perspective of each author.

Teaching Suggestions:

- Encourage students to read actively. Circling words, writing questions in the margins, and taking notes are three ways in which students can make reading a more active and meaningful experience.

- Make sure students know how to use the vocabulary glosses, *Culture and Language Notes*, and other support tools to assist them in the reading process.

- Encourage students to use context to guess the meaning of unfamiliar words.

- Play the recorded version of the reading passage and ask students to listen to how the reader groups words together. As they listen to the recording, students can lightly underline or circle the groups of words.

4. After You Read: Understanding the Text (30 to 45 minutes)

Following each reading, there are two post-reading activities that give students the chance to (a) clarify their understanding of the text, and (b) discuss the issues raised in the reading. The comprehension questions are for students to work through on their own. Questions in the *Consider the Issues* section, on the other hand, ask students to talk about ideas introduced in the reading.

Teaching Suggestions:

- Get students to discuss their reactions to the readings in pairs or groups. The process of discussing questions and answers gives students an opportunity to check their comprehension more critically and analyze their reactions to the passages.

- Show students the value of returning to the reading again and again to answer the comprehension and discussion questions. Ask them to point out the specific places in the reading where they have found answers to the questions posed.

- If time permits and you would like students to have additional writing practice, ask them to write an essay or a journal entry on one of the questions in the *Consider the Issues* section.

5. Reading Skills (20 to 30 minutes)

At the beginning of each *Reading Skills* section, students encounter a short explanation of the skill in focus and, when appropriate, an example of how that skill relates to the reading in the chapter. The task following this explanation asks students to return to the reading to think about and apply a new reading skill.

Teaching Suggestions:

- Discuss the general purpose of developing reading skills. The more students understand the rationale behind acquiring these critical skills, the more motivated they will be to develop and refine them.

- Review the explanations and sample sentences at the beginning of each *Reading Skills* section before asking students to tackle the questions that follow. Encourage them to ask any questions they have about the explanations or examples.

- Reflect with students on the ways in which they can apply the reading skills they have learned in each chapter to other reading passages and to other reading genres.

6. Building Vocabulary (20 to 30 minutes)

Reading extensively is an excellent way for students to increase their vocabulary base. Considering this, we pay careful attention to developing students' vocabulary-building skills in each chapter of **Select Readings**. Understanding phrasal verbs, working with word forms, finding synonyms, and a variety of other vocabulary-building skills are taught throughout the book. Like the reading skill activities, each *Building Vocabulary* section starts out with a short explanation and, when appropriate, examples of the skill in focus. In the activity that follows the explanation, students typically scan the reading to gather and analyze various types of words.

Teaching Suggestions:

- Review the explanations and sample sentences at the beginning of each *Building Vocabulary* section before asking students to tackle the questions that follow. Encourage them to ask any questions they have about the explanations or examples.

- Show students the value of returning to the reading to find an answer whenever they are unsure of a vocabulary-related question.

- Encourage students to keep a vocabulary notebook. Present various ways in which students can organize the words in their notebook: by chapter, by topic, by part of speech, etc.

- Discuss the value of using an English-English learner's dictionary to find the meanings of unfamiliar words.

7. Language Focus (20 to 30 minutes)

The final skill-building section in each chapter calls attention to important grammatical structures and functions that occur with some degree of frequency in the reading passage. The goal of this section is to focus students' attention on critical grammar points as they occur in context.

Teaching Suggestions:

- Review the explanations and sample sentences at the beginning of each *Language Focus* section before asking students to tackle the questions that follow. Encourage students to ask any questions they have about the explanations or examples.

- Invite students to talk about what they already know about the language point in focus. Many students know a great deal about grammar and are pleased to demonstrate this knowledge.

- Underscore the fact that the *Language Focus* sections are intended to help students review language they have already learned in the context of an authentic reading passage. It can be very valuable for students to see the ways in which grammatical structures they have studied appear naturally in real-life reading selections.

8. Discussion and Writing (45 to 60 minutes)

At the end of each chapter, students have an opportunity to talk and write about a variety of issues. The questions in this section provide students with a chance to broaden their view on the topic of the reading and to address more global issues and concerns.

Teaching Suggestions:

- When time permits, let students discuss a question a second time with a different partner or group. This allows them to apply what they learned in their first discussion of the question.

- Choose one or more of the questions in this section as an essay topic for students.

Bonus Features

Crossword Puzzles. At the end of each chapter, you will find a crossword puzzle that recycles and reviews some of the key vocabulary from the reading. These puzzles can be used as homework, as optional activities for groups or individuals who finish other exercises early, or as review activities several weeks after completing a chapter.

Maps. Each location mentioned in a reading passage is clearly marked on one of the maps found on pages 169–173.

This project grew out of our deep and profound love for reading, and for sharing this love of reading with our students. In developing **Select Readings,** we have enjoyed the process of talking to teachers all over the world about they types of authentic selections they feel their students enjoy the most, and learn the most from. We hope that you and your students enjoy teaching and learning with **Select Readings.**

Jean Bernard
Linda Lee

Chapter 1 What Is Creative Thinking?

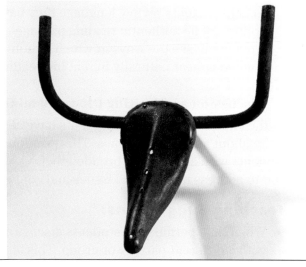

Picasso's *Head of Bull*

> *Creative minds have always been known to survive any kind of bad training.*
>
> —Anna Freud
> *Psychoanalyst*
> *(1895–1982)*

Chapter Focus

CONTENT:
Suggestions for learning to think creatively

READING SKILL:
Identifying main ideas

BUILDING VOCABULARY:
Figures of speech

LANGUAGE FOCUS:
Noun clauses

Before You Read

1. Look at the title of the article on page 4. What are some possible answers to the question, "What is creative thinking?" Give an example of someone who thinks creatively.

2. In your opinion, is it important for people to learn to think creatively? Does it help people be more successful? Why or why not?

3. The figure below can be seen in three different ways. Which ways can you see? Can you see something different as well? How is this an example of creative thinking?

If you look at it one way, it's a bird. If you look at it another way, it could be a question mark. If you turn it upside down, it looks like a seal juggling a ball on its nose.

WHAT IS CREATIVE THINKING?

by Roger von Oech

from *A Whack on the Side of the Head:
How You Can Be More Creative*

*Note: Explanations for words in **blue** type can be found in the
Culture and Language Notes on pages 150–168.*

1   I once asked advertising legend[1] **Carl Ally** what makes the
creative person tick.[2] Ally responded, "The creative person wants to
be a know-it-all. He wants to know about all kinds of things: ancient
history, nineteenth century mathematics, current manufacturing
5   techniques, flower arranging, and hog futures.[3] Because he never
knows when these ideas might come together to form a new idea. It
may happen six minutes later or six years down the road. But he has
faith that it will happen."

      I agree wholeheartedly. Knowledge is the stuff from which new
10   ideas are made. Nonetheless, knowledge alone won't make a person
creative. I think that we've all known people who knew lots of facts
and nothing creative happened. Their knowledge just sat in their
crania[4] because they didn't think about what they knew in any new
ways. The real key to being creative lies in what you do with your
15   knowledge.

      Creative thinking requires an attitude that allows you to search for
ideas and manipulate your knowledge and experience.[5] With this
outlook,[6] you try various approaches, first one, then another, often
not getting anywhere. You use crazy, foolish, and impractical ideas as
20   stepping stones to practical new ideas. You break the rules
occasionally, and explore for ideas in unusual outside places. In

---

[1] **advertising legend**   a person who has become famous in the field of
advertising

[2] **make a person tick**   what makes a person behave the way he or she does

[3] **futures**   shares in the stock market that are bought or sold in advance
of delivery

[4] **crania**   skulls (plural form of *cranium*)

[5] **manipulate your knowledge and experience**   use your knowledge
and experience in different ways

[6] **outlook**   point of view

short, by adopting a creative outlook you open yourself up both to new possibilities and to change.

A good example of a person who did this is **Johann Gutenberg**. What Gutenberg did was combine two previously unconnected ideas: the wine press and the coin punch. The purpose of the coin punch was to leave an image on a small area such as a gold coin. The function of the wine press was, and still is, to apply force over a large area to squeeze the juice out of grapes. One day, Gutenberg, perhaps after he'd drunk a goblet or two of wine, playfully asked himself, "What if I took a bunch of these coin punches and put them under the force of the wine press so that they left their image on paper?" The resulting combination was the printing press and **movable type**.

Navy Admiral[7] **Grace Hopper** had the task of explaining the meaning of a nanosecond to some non-technical computer users. (A nanosecond is a billionth of a second, and it's the basic time interval of a supercomputer's internal clock.) She wondered, "How can I get them to understand the brevity of a nanosecond? Why not look at it as a space problem rather than a time problem? I'll just use the distance light travels in one billionth of a second." She pulled out a piece of string 30 centimeters long (11.8 inches) and told her visitors, "Here is one nanosecond."

In 1792, the musicians of **Franz Joseph Haydn's** orchestra got mad because the Duke promised them a vacation, but continually postponed it. They asked Haydn to talk to the **Duke** about getting some time off. Haydn thought for a bit, decided to let music do the talking, and then wrote the "Farewell Symphony." The performance began with a full orchestra, but as the piece went along, it was scored[8] to need fewer and fewer instruments. As each musician finished his part, he blew out his candle and left the stage. They did this, one by one, until the stage was empty. The Duke got the message and gave them a vacation.

Then there's **Pablo Picasso**. One day, he went outside his house and found an old bicycle. He looked at it for a little bit and took off the seat and the handle bars. Then he welded them together to create the head of a bull.

Each of these examples illustrates the creative mind's power to transform one thing into another. By changing perspective and playing with our knowledge, we can make the ordinary extraordinary and the

---

[7] **Navy Admiral** an officer of very high rank in the navy who commands a group of ships

[8] **scored** written in musical notation format with specific parts for each instrument

60 unusual commonplace. In this way, wine presses squeeze out information, string is transformed into nanoseconds, labor grievances become symphonies, and bicycle seats turn into bulls' heads.

The **Nobel Prize** winning physician **Albert Szent-Györgyi** put it well[9] when he said: Discovery consists of looking at the same thing as
65 everyone else and thinking something different.

Here are two quick exercises to give you a chance to "think something different."

Exercise 1: An eccentric[10] old king wants to give his throne to one of his two sons. He decides that a horse race will be run and the son who owns the slower horse will become king. The sons, each fearing
70 that the other will cheat by having his horse run less fast than it is capable, ask the **court fool** for his advice. With only two words the fool tells them how to make sure that the race will be fair. What are the two words?

75 **Exercise 2:** Can you think of a way in which you put a sheet of newspaper on the floor so that when two people stand face to face on it, they won't be able to touch one another? Cutting or tearing the paper is not allowed. Neither is tying up the people or preventing them from moving.

80 Why don't we "think something different" more often? There are several main reasons. The first is that we don't need to be creative for most of what we do. For example, we don't need to be creative when we're driving on the freeway,[11] or riding in an elevator, or waiting in line at a grocery store. We are creatures of habit when it comes to the
85 business of living—everything from doing paperwork to tying our shoes to haggling[12] with telephone solicitors.

For most of our activities, these routines are indispensable. Without them, our lives would be in chaos, and we wouldn't get much accomplished. If you got up this morning and started contemplating
90 the bristles on your toothbrush or questioning the meaning of toast, you probably wouldn't make it to work. Staying on routine thought paths enables us to do the many things we need to do without having to think about them.

---

[9] **put it well**   expressed the idea well; made the point

[10] **eccentric**   having some strange or unusual ideas or ways of doing things

[11] **freeway**   a large highway with no tolls

[12] **haggling**   arguing, usually over money

Another reason we're not more creative is that we haven't been
95   taught to be. Much of our educational system is an elaborate game of
"guess what the teacher is thinking." Many of us have been taught to
think that the best ideas are in someone else's head. How many of
your teachers asked you, "What original ideas do you have?"

There are times, however, when you need to be creative and
100   generate new ways to accomplish your objectives. When this
happens, your own belief systems may prevent you from doing so.
Here we come to a third reason why we don't "think something
different" more often. Most of us have certain attitudes that lock our
thinking into the status quo[13] and keep us thinking "more of the
105   same." These attitudes are necessary for most of what we do, but
they can get in the way when we're trying to be creative.

About the Source

From *A Whack on the Side of the Head: How You Can be More
Creative* by Roger von Oech. This best-selling book has been praised
by business leaders, educators, artists, and anyone hoping to unlock
the power of the mind to think creatively. It has been translated into
11 languages and used in seminars around the world.

After You Read

Understanding the Text

A. Multiple choice. For each item below, circle the best answer.

1. The main purpose of the reading is to _____.

    a. explain how the printing press was invented

    b. teach readers how to think creatively

    c. explain why Haydn wrote the "Farewell Symphony"

    d. criticize teachers and educational systems

---

[13] **status quo**   (from Latin) the way things are

2. According to the author, people who think creatively do all of the following, except _____.

    a. contemplate the bristles on their toothbrushes

    b. try to learn everything they can about a wide range of topics

    c. look at the same thing as everyone else and think something different

    d. use crazy, foolish, and impractical ideas

3. The examples given by the author show the power of the creative mind to _____.

    a. transform one thing into another in an original way

    b. give the correct answers to exercises

    c. ask their teachers what they are thinking

    d. stay on routine thought paths

4. By giving readers some quick exercises to do, the author gives them an opportunity to _____.

    a. learn some interesting facts

    b. argue with his main point

    c. question the meaning of life

    d. think something different

5. The author would probably approve of teachers who _____.

    a. ask students about their original ideas

    b. have students guess what they are thinking

    c. give students more knowledge

    d. transfer their own attitudes to students

6. The overall tone of the reading is _____.

    a. serious

    b. sad

    c. entertaining

    d. angry

B. Consider the issues. Work with a partner to answer the questions below.

1. The author claims that through creative thinking, "we can make the ordinary extraordinary and the unusual commonplace." Give one example from the reading of how an ordinary thing was made into something extraordinary. Give another example of how something unusual was made into something commonplace.

2. Try to think of possible solutions to Exercises 1 and 2 (lines 68–79). Compare your solutions with the ones at the bottom of this page. Did these exercises encourage you to think creatively? Explain how.

3. The author claims that most people do not think creatively because they have not learned to do so in school. Do you agree? In your experience, do teachers ask about their students' original ideas? Should they?

Reading Skill

Identifying main ideas

In a typical piece of writing, the author expresses two or three **main ideas,** or general messages about a topic. These ideas may be restated several times in order to make sure the reader understands them clearly.

Which of the following statements express the author's main ideas about creative thinking? Check (√) them.

1. _____ Carl Ally is an advertising legend who thinks creatively.

2. __√__ Creative thinking requires people to look at things in a new way.

3. _____ The real key to being creative lies in what you do with your knowledge.

4. _____ In short, by adopting a creative outlook you open yourself up both to new possibilities and change.

5. _____ The purpose of the coin punch was to leave an image on a small area such as a gold coin.

6. _____ A nanosecond is a billionth of a second.

7. _____ As each musician finished his part, he blew out his candle and left the stage.

8. _____ By changing perspective and playing with our knowledge, we can make the ordinary extraordinary and the unusual commonplace.

1. The two words are: switch horses. (That way, each brother will try to *win* the race, riding on the other brother's horse.) 2. Try putting the newspaper in a doorway—door closed—with the two people standing on each side.

Figures of speech

A **figure of speech** is a way of using words creatively. Some figures of speech (metaphors and similes) make a comparison between two unlikely things.

He has a *heart of stone.*
She can run *like the wind.*

Another type of **figure of speech** gives human traits to non-human things:

The *moonlight danced* on the surface of the water.

A. Choose the best interpretation of the figures of speech (in **boldface**) in these sentences from the reading. Use context to help you understand the meaning of the term. Cirle the letter of your answer.

1. Knowledge is **the stuff** from which new ideas are made.

   a. the hardware

   b. the raw material

   c. the creativity

2. You use crazy, foolish, and impractical ideas as **stepping stones** to practical new ideas.

   a. answers to problems

   b. keys to happiness

   c. ways to achieve a goal

3. We are creatures of habit when it comes to **the business** of living—everything from doing paperwork to tying our shoes to haggling with telephone solicitors.

   a. profession or occupation

   b. the process or activity

   c. the topic or subject

B. Reread the author's story about Franz Joseph Haydn's orchestra (lines 43–52). Then answer the questions below.

1. The composer decided to "let music do the talking." What did the orchestra want to say to the Duke?

_____

_____

2. In line 50, each musician's act of blowing out his candle sent a special message to the Duke. What does the candle stand for? What did the act of blowing it out communicate to the Duke?

_____

_____

Language Focus

Noun clauses

A **noun clause** is part of a sentence that takes the place of a noun. Like all clauses, a noun clause has its own subject and verb. Noun clauses usually begin with words *that, what, why, which,* or *how.* Writers use noun clauses in complex sentences that combine information or ideas.

I asked him *what makes the creative person tick.*

A. Underline the noun clauses in the following sentences.

1. People didn't think about what they knew in any new ways.

2. The real key to being creative lies in what you do with your knowledge.

3. What Gutenberg did was to combine two previously unconnected ideas.

4. Another reason we're not more creative is that we have not been taught to be.

B. Use noun clauses of your own to complete these statements about the reading.

1. The most interesting thing I learned from the reading is that

_____

2. I am still not sure about how _____

_____

3. I would like to ask the author why _____

_____

Discussion & Writing

1. The author of *A Whack on the Side of the Head* is president of a consulting firm that has conducted creativity seminars for many international companies. Why do you think they are interested in his ideas? Do you find his ideas interesting? Why or why not?

2. In the same book, the author uses the following anecdote (short story from personal experience) to make a point. Read the story and write a sentence or two explaining the meaning of it.

> A creativity teacher invited one of his students over to his house for tea. They talked for a bit, and then came time for tea. The teacher poured some into the student's cup. Even after the cup was full, he continued to pour. The cup overflowed and tea spilled out onto the floor.

> Finally, the student said: "Master, you must stop pouring; the tea is overflowing—it's not going into the cup."

> The teacher replied, "That's very observant. The same is true with you. If you are to receive any of my teachings, you must first empty out what you have in your mental cup."

3. **Group work.** Work with several classmates to think creatively about one of the tasks below. Come up with a plan or solution on paper. Present your ideas to the whole class.

a. Design a machine or device that would make your life easier or more fun (for example, an electric page-turner, a personal air transporter).

b. Create a piece of art from two pieces of junk, such as part of an old computer or TV and an automobile tire.

c. Think of an unusual yet effective way to send someone an important message.

Crossword Puzzle

Use words from the reading to complete the crossword puzzle.

Across:

3 Important part of a bicycle

4 The _____ Prize

8 Point of view

10 To argue

11 Small hairs on a toothbrush

12 The stuff from which new ideas are made

14 Commanding officer in the Navy

15 The _____ quo

16 One cranium, many _____.

2 Famous European artist

5 Carl Ally was an advertising _____.

6 A fast, wide road with many lanes

7 The two words the fool said were, "switch _____."

9 Having strange or unusual ideas

10 Composer of the "Farewell Symphony"

13 To change one thing into another

Down:

1 One billionth of a second

Chapter ▲

2 Why I Quit the Company

*Work is good,
provided you do
not forget to live.*

—*Bantu proverb*

Chapter Focus

CONTENT:
Explanation of an employee's decision
to resign

READING SKILL:
Distinguishing fact from opinion

BUILDING VOCABULARY:
Phrasal verbs

LANGUAGE FOCUS:
Past conditional sentences

Before You Read

1. What are your career goals? How do you expect to achieve them?

2. Read the title of the article and then take one minute to skim the text. What do you think the article will be about? Share your answers with a partner.

3. In today's busy world, people seem to have less time to spend with friends and family. What types of problems might this cause? Do you think it is more important to "live to work" or "work to live"? Explain why.

Reading Passage

WHY I QUIT THE COMPANY

by Tomoyuki Iwashita

from *The New Internationalist*

1   When I tell people that I quit working for the company after only a year, most of them think I'm crazy. They can't understand why I would want to give up a prestigious and secure job. But I think I'd have been crazy to stay, and I'll try to explain why.

5   I started working for the company immediately after graduating from university. It's a big, well-known trading company with about 6,000 employees all over the world. There's a lot of competition to get into this and other similar companies, which promise young people a wealthy and successful future. I was set on course to be a 10 Japanese "**yuppie**."

I'd been used to living independently as a student, looking after myself[1] and organizing my own schedule. As soon as I started working all that changed. I was given a room in the company dormitory, which

---

[1] **looking after myself**   taking care of myself

is like a fancy hotel, with a 24-hour hot bath service and all meals laid
15 on.[2] Most single company employees live in a dormitory like this, and
many married employees live in company apartments. The dorm
system is actually a great help because living in Tokyo costs more than
young people can afford—but I found it stifling.[3]

My life rapidly became reduced to a shuttle between[4] the dorm and
20 the office. The working day is officially eight hours, but you can never
leave the office on time. I used to work from nine in the morning until
eight or nine at night, and often until midnight. Drinking with
colleagues after work is part of the job; you can't say no. The company
building contained cafeterias, shops, a bank, a post office, a doctor's
25 office, a barber's… I never needed to leave the building. Working,
drinking, sleeping, and standing on a horribly crowded commuter
train for an hour and a half each way: This was my life. I spent all my
time with the same colleagues; when I wasn't involved in entertaining
clients on the weekend, I was expected to play golf with my
30 colleagues. I soon lost sight of the world outside the company.

This isolation is part of the brainwashing process.[5] A personnel
manager said: "We want excellent students who are active, clever,
and tough. Three months is enough to train them to be devoted
businessmen." I would hear my colleagues saying: "I'm not making
35 any profit for the company, so I'm not contributing." Very few
employees claim all the overtime pay due to them. Keeping an
employee costs the company 50 million **yen** ($400,000) a year, or so
the company claims. Many employees put the company's profits
before their own mental and physical well-being.

40 Overtiredness and overwork leave you little energy to analyze or
criticize your situation. There are shops full of "health drinks,"
cocktails of caffeine and other drugs, which will keep you going even
when you're exhausted. *Karoshi* (death from overwork) is
increasingly common and is always being discussed in the
45 newspapers. I myself collapsed from working too hard. My boss told
me: "You should control your health; it's your own fault if you get
sick." There is no paid sick leave;[6] I used up half of my fourteen days'
annual leave[7] because of sickness.

---

[2] **laid on**   provided without charge; free
[3] **stifling**   difficult to live in; oppressive
[4] **shuttle between**   repeated travel back and forth over the same route
[5] **brainwashing process**   program designed to force people to accept new beliefs; indoctrination
[6] **sick leave**   time allowed away from work because of illness
[7] **annual leave**   time permitted away from work each year for any reason, usually vacation

We had a **labor union**, but it seemed to have an odd relationship
50 with the management. A couple of times a year I was told to go home
at five o'clock. The union representatives were coming around to
investigate working hours; everyone knew in advance. If it was
"discovered" that we were all working overtime in excess of fifty
hours a month our boss might have had some problem being
55 promoted; and our prospects[8] would have been affected. So we all
pretended to work normal hours that day.

The company also controls its employees' private lives. Many
company employees under thirty are single. They are expected to
devote all their time to the company and become good workers; they
60 don't have time to find a girlfriend. The company offers scholarships
to the most promising young employees to enable them to study
abroad for a year or two. But unmarried people who are on these
courses are not allowed to get married until they have completed the
course! Married employees who are sent to train abroad have to leave
65 their families in Japan for the first year.

In fact, the quality of married life is often determined by the
husband's work. Men who have just gotten married try to go home
early for a while, but soon have to revert to the norm of late-night
work. They have little time to spend with their wives and even on the
70 weekend are expected to play golf with colleagues. Fathers cannot
find time to communicate with their children and child rearing is
largely left to mothers. Married men posted abroad will often leave
their family behind in Japan; they fear that their children will fall
behind in the fiercely competitive[9] **Japanese education system**.

75 Why do people put up with this? They believe this to be a normal
working life or just cannot see an alternative. Many think that such
personal sacrifices are necessary to keep Japan economically
successful. Perhaps, saddest of all, Japan's education and
socialization[10] processes do not equip people with the intellectual
80 and spiritual resources to question and challenge the status quo.[11]
They stamp out even the desire for a different kind of life.

However, there are some signs that things are changing. Although
many new employees in my company were quickly brainwashed,
many others, like myself, complained about life in the company and
85 seriously considered leaving. But most of them were already in

---

[8] **prospects**   chances for advancement

[9] **fiercely competitive**   very competitive; involving people trying to be
more successful than others

[10] **socialization**   the process of learning to adapt to the rules of a society

[11] **challenge the status quo**   dare to question the way things are

fetters of debt.[12] Pleased with themselves for getting into the company and anticipating[13] a life of executive luxury, these new employees throw their money around. Every night they are out drinking. They buy smart clothes and take a taxi back to the 90 dormitory after the last train has gone. They start borrowing money from the bank and soon they have a debt growing like a snowball rolling down a slope.[14] The banks demand no security for loans; it's enough to be working for a well-known company. Some borrow as much as a year's salary in the first few months. They can't leave the 95 company while they have such debts to pay off.

I was one of the few people in my intake of employees[15] who didn't get into debt. I left the company dormitory after three months to share an apartment with a friend. I left the company exactly one year after I entered it. It took me a while to find a new job, but I'm 100 working as a journalist now. My life is still busy, but it's a lot better than it was. I'm lucky because nearly all big Japanese companies are like the one I worked for, and conditions in many small companies are even worse.

It's not easy to opt out of a lifestyle that is generally considered to 105 be prestigious[16] and desirable, but more and more young people in Japan are thinking about doing it. You have to give up a lot of superficially attractive[17] material benefits in order to preserve the quality of your life and your sanity. I don't think I was crazy to leave the company. I think I would have gone crazy if I'd stayed.

About the Author

Tomoyuki Iwashita is a freelance writer now living in Paris with his wife, Michelle.

---

[12] **fetters of debt**   restraints on one's freedom caused by owing money

[13] **anticipating**   looking forward to

[14] **like a snowball rolling down a slope**   very, very quickly

[15] **intake of employees**   group of new workers hired at the same time

[16] **prestigious**   respected or admired because of success or high quality

[17] **superficially attractive**   pleasing, but only on the surface

After You Read

Understanding the Text

A. Events in the story.

1. Order the events. Number the events in "Why I Quit the Company" from the first (1) to the last (9).

   _____ After three months, he left the dormitory to share an apartment with a friend.

   _____ He graduated from university.

   _____ He found a new job as a journalist.

   _____ As a student, Tomoyuki Iwashita lived independently.

   _____ As soon as he started work, he moved to the company dormitory and commuted to work.

   _____ He has a busy life now, but feels happier.

   _____ While he was living in the dorm, he worked very hard during the week and played golf with colleagues on the weekends.

   _____ He quit the company after one year.

   _____ Immediately after that, he started working for a large trading company.

2. Check (√) which of the following were NOT part of Mr. Iwashita's life as a company man.

   _____ commuting for an hour and a half each day

   _____ falling into debt

   _____ collapsing from working too hard

   _____ taking a lot of paid sick leave

   _____ playing golf with clients

B. Consider the issues. Work with a partner to answer the questions below.

1. Do you think the writer is happy he quit the company? Find at least two lines in the article that support your answer.

2. Would you like to work for the company described in the article? Explain why or why not.

Distinguishing fact from opinion
A statement of **fact** relates something that the writer knows to be true.

> The dorm system is actually a great help because **living in Tokyo costs more than young people can afford.**

In narrative writing (writing that tells a personal story), expressions of the writer's **opinion** are sometimes added to the facts.

> —but **I found it stifling.**

A. Fact or Opinion? Read the statements from the article and write F if it is a statement of fact or O if it is an opinion.

___F___ **1.** I started working for the company immediately after graduating from university.

_____ **2.** There's a lot of competition to get into this and other similar companies.

_____ **3.** I was set on course to be a Japanese "yuppie."

_____ **4.** The working day is officially eight hours.

_____ **5.** Very few employees claim all the overtime pay due to them.

_____ **6.** Many company employees under thirty are single.

_____ **7.** My life is still busy, but it's a lot better than it was.

_____ **8.** I think I would have gone crazy if I'd stayed.

B. Check (√) the opinions you think Tomoyuki Iwashita would agree with. Then tell a partner whether you agree or disagree.

1. _____ Entertaining clients on the weekends is great fun.

2. _____ Family life in Japan suffers because companies overwork their employees.

3. _____ More workers should question the status quo.

Phrasal verbs
Phrasal verbs have two or three parts: a verb and one or two other words like *down, up, in, out, after, with,* or *of.* Many phrasal verbs have a meaning that is different from the verbs by themselves:

Where did you *put* the keys?

Why do people *put up with* this treatment? (Why do they tolerate it?)

The best way to understand a phrasal verb is to try and guess its meaning from the context of the sentence. If you are still not sure, a good dictionary lists many phrasal verbs and their definitions along with the main verb.

A. Underline the phrasal verbs in the sentences below. Then use context to guess the meaning of each verb. Share your answers with a partner.

1. I'd been used to living independently as a student, looking after myself and organizing my own schedule.

2. There is no paid sick leave; I used up half of my fourteen days' annual leave because of sickness.

3. Japan's education and socialization processes stamp out even the desire for a different kind of life.

4. They can't leave the company while they have such debts to pay off.

5. It's not easy to opt out of a lifestyle that is generally considered to be prestigious and desirable, but more and more young people in Japan are thinking about doing it.

6. You have to give up a lot of superficially attractive material benefits in order to preserve the quality of your life and your sanity.

B. Use a phrasal verb from the reading to answer each question below.

1. Why didn't Mr. Iwashita like having everything provided for him by the company?

2. Why is it difficult for employees who spend too much money to leave the company?

3. According to Mr. Iwashita, what are a lot of young people in Japan thinking about doing?

Past conditional sentences

A **past conditional** sentence describes something that was not true or did not happen in the past. These sentences contain a clause beginning with *if...* (states the imaginative condition), and a main clause (explains the result of that condition).

> *If I had stayed*, I would have gone crazy.

Past conditional sentences have an unusual verb structure:

Conditional Clause		Main Clause
If + past perfect +	$\begin{cases} should \\ would \\ could \\ might \end{cases}$	+ *have* + past participle

A. The following paragraph describes what might have happened if Mr. Iwashita had not quit the company. Fill in the missing words.

If he had not quit the company, he would have (1)_____ crazy. He would still be working from nine in the morning until eight or nine at night, and often until midnight. If he had (2) _____ with the company, he could have (3) _____ golf with his colleagues every weekend. If he (4) _____ been lucky, he might have received a scholarship to study abroad for a year or two. If he had been married, he (5) _____ have been expected to leave his family in Japan.

B. Think about something significant that happened in your past (for example, a move to another city or town, a change of schools, taking or leaving a job). Write three past conditional sentences based on this experience. Read your sentences to a partner.

> If my family hadn't moved to New York, I wouldn't have met my best friend.

1. _____

2. _____

3. _____

1. **Group work.** Discuss the following questions with a small group of your classmates. Share your group's responses with the class.

   a. What would you have done in Mr. Iwashita's position? Would you have quit the company, too? Explain why or why not.

   b. Imagine you have been offered a job at a large, prestigious company. What questions would you want to ask your prospective employer before you accept the offer? Add to the list below.

   What are the working hours?

   Does the company provide transportation to and from work?

2. What do you think is more important, work or family? Write a paragraph explaining the reasons for your choice. The first sentence should clearly state your opinion, and the remaining sentences should support your main idea.

Crossword Puzzle

Use words from the reading to complete the crossword puzzle.

Across:

1 Some things are hard to put _____ with.

4 Given free of charge (two words)

6 A building where many people live

8 Give back the money you owe (two words)

10 Co-workers

11 Young urban professional

13 More than the usual number of hours worked

14 Like a _____ rolling down a slope

Down:

1 An organization that protects workers

2 Out of one's mind

3 The author chose to _____ out of the company lifestyle.

5 Chances for advancement

7 Japanese word meaning "death from overwork"

8 Very respectable

9 _____ (chains) of debt

11 Unit of currency in Japan

12 Time taken away from work

3 The Body Shop

With his new chest, teenager Sean McCormack can play all his favorite sports except football.

*You must do the
thing you think
you cannot do.*

—*Eleanor Roosevelt*
Humanitarian and diplomat
(1884–1962)

Chapter Focus

CONTENT:
Using tissue engineering to repair the
human body

READING SKILL:
Inferencing

BUILDING VOCABULARY:
Using context to guess meaning

LANGUAGE FOCUS:
Modals of possibility

Before You Read

1. Read the first paragraph of the article below. What does the doctor believe he can do? What do you think rest of the article will be about?

2. Give one example of how the practice of medicine has changed in the last 100 years. How do you think it will change 100 years from now? What do you hope doctors will be able to do that they can't do now?

3. The photo on the right shows a human ear that has been created in a medical laboratory. How could the process of creating human organs be used to help people?

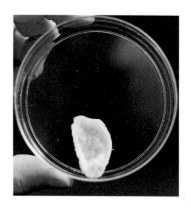

Reading Passage

THE BODY SHOP

by Charles Hirschberg

from *Life* magazine

1   "I believe I can build a human liver," proclaims an exhausted Dr. Joseph Vacanti, collapsing into his office chair at Children's Hospital in Boston.

There's something disquieting about hearing a doctor say such a
5   thing. One can't help thinking of the ghastly monster created by **Dr. Frankenstein**, with its translucent[1] yellow skin, shriveled face and black misshapen lips.

But Dr. Vacanti is no Dr. Frankenstein. Still in his scrubs, he has just come from the operating room where he performed lifesaving
10   surgery on an infant. His body is spent; but his eyes flash with energy as he talks about his dreams. "It has never seemed like science fiction

---

[1] **translucent**   partially transparent

to me," says Vacanti, a professor of surgery at Harvard Medical School and Massachusetts General Hospital. "My professional goal is to solve the problem of vital organ[2] shortage." More than 50,000
15 Americans are currently in need of organ transplant, and 4,000 of them are likely to die before a donor[3] is located. Vacanti's solution is simple: Instead of replacing a faltering organ with one harvested from someone else, why not take a few healthy cells from the sick person and grow him or her a new one? Such an organ would probably work
20 better, too, since the body is less likely to reject tissue made of its own genetic material.

It sounds too good to be true. But it's beginning to look like it just might work. And if it does, tissue regeneration could revolutionize the practice of medicine.

25 **Apothecaries** have experimented with tissue replacement for centuries: As early as the sixth century B.C., **Hindu surgeons** began using arm skin to repair mangled noses. It wasn't until the late 1970s that John Burke of Massachusetts General and Ioannis Yannas of the Massachusetts Institute of Technology succeeded in growing skin in a
30 laboratory. Recently, several brands of artificial skin have been approved by the **Food and Drug Administration** for treatment of ulcers and severe burns.

Still, as an organized field of inquiry, with an international professional society and a journal to report its progress, the science
35 of tissue engineering has been around for little more than a decade. There is quite a difference between growing a relatively simple organ such as skin and growing a complex one like a liver. For the liver is a congeries[4] of many different types of tissues, all of which work together to accomplish a host of complicated tasks. "When I started
40 trying to do this," says Vacanti, 49, the son of a Nebraska dental surgeon, "a lot of people thought I was crazy. Some still think so."

Not John and Debra McCormack of Norwood, Massachusetts. Regardless of whether Vacanti succeeds in building a liver, he has already made a tremendous difference in the life of their 17-year-old
45 son, Sean.

"When Sean was born, I was terrified," Debra recalls. The boy suffered from a rare condition called Poland's syndrome. A large portion of his chest wall was either missing or deformed. His heart was

---

[2] **vital organ** an organ (such as the heart or liver) which the human body cannot live without

[3] **donor** person who agrees to donate their organs to someone in need

[4] **congeries** a collection of different things

healthy enough, but it lay unusually far to the right and was so
completely unprotected by bone or muscle that it could be seen beating
through his skin. Nevertheless, Sean grew to be a tough, resilient kid[5]
and a fine athlete. "My life never revolved around Poland's syndrome,"
he says. But he was embarrassed by his sunken chest and refused to
take his shirt off in public—a problem, his parents knew, that could
have increasingly serious implications as he grew older. What's more, it
was often a torment to watch Sean play baseball, talented **pitcher**
though he was. His parents still wince remembering the day he was hit
by a **line drive** just inches from his exposed heart. Sean shook off the
sting[6] and proceeded to win the game, but by this time both he and his
parents were anxious to see what could be done about his condition.
That's what brought them to Children's Hospital.

Surgeon Dennis Lund first proposed tissue engineering in 1993.
"I'd worked with Dr. Vacanti for years," Lund says, "and I explained to
Sean and his father that we had a brand new technology in the
laboratory. It had never been used in humans before, but I thought it
would be completely safe because we would be using Sean's own
tissue." It took a long time for the McCormacks to fully comprehend
what was being suggested. ("The first thing we did," recalls John
McCormack, "was go to the dictionary and look up the word
protocol"—which turned out to be governmentese[7] for *experiment*.)
But after much study and many questions, they got the basic idea:
Surgeons would open up Sean's chest and extract a piece of
unneeded cartilage[8] from his malformed sternum.[9] Next, a disk about
the size of a doorknob made of a specially designed polymer[10] would
be fashioned to fill the hole in the boy's chest. Then, in Vacanti's
laboratory, Sean's cartilage cells would be dropped like seeds onto
the disk and nourished in a kind of soup laced with growth media
(substances that encourage cells to reproduce). When a sufficient
number of cells developed, the disk would be surgically implanted in
Sean's chest. The cells would continue to grow inside his body, and as
they did, the polymer disk would gradually dissolve. After three
months, if everything went right, the disk would be completely gone,
and in its place would be healthy, living cartilage.

---

[5] **a tough, resilient kid**   a young person who is able to recover quickly
from illness or injury

[6] **shook off the sting**   ignored the pain

[7] **governmentese**   official language that uses complicated terms for
ordinary ones

[8] **cartilage**   tough elastic tissue found, for example, in the nose and ear

[9] **sternum**   breastbone

[10] **polymer**   scientific term for a material with a specific molecular structure

Sean was glib[11] about all of this: "I'm a guinea pig,[12] huh?" But
85 when his parents told him the decision was his, he never hesitated.
Four surgeries later, Sean is equally glib about being the first human
in history with a tissue-engineered chest. "Sorta cool,"[13] he says,
smiling. But his parents are gleeful. Debra says it makes her
indescribably happy to watch her son saunter around with no shirt on
90 in front of his peers." Sean has given up baseball in favor of **BMX
bike racing** ("I don't do anything crazy," he claims, though he doesn't
hesitate to fly off ramps at outrageous speeds). In short, says his
sister, Kelly "he's my 17-year-old brother who rides around town and
does 17-year-old things." Which is precisely what his doctors had
95 hoped to achieve.

Though Sean's doctors preach caution, "We'll want to continue to
monitor him," says Vacanti, "probably for the rest of his life," they can
scarcely hide their enthusiasm as they dream up other applications of
the procedure. "The possibilities are phenomenal," says Dr. Joseph
100 Upton, who did Sean's reconstructive surgery. "For example, I see a lot
of patients who have facial paralysis.[14] Boy, it sure would be nice if we
could repair them with muscle from their own tissue. Right now it's pie
in the sky,[15] but believe me, in five or ten years it won't be. And today I
was working on a kid who was in a motorcycle accident and lost an
105 awful lot of bone. Supposing we could repair that with a kind of
injectable bone, instead of doing the huge amounts of bone grafts[16] we
have to do now? I think we will see such a product before too long."

About the	**Source**	

Life magazine was started by the American publisher Henry Luce in
1936 as a weekly magazine that reported national and international
events through the eyes of outstanding photographers and reporters.
Today, the magazine is published only as special editions that focus on
a specific topic. "The Body Shop" is from a special issue published in
1998 about medical breakthroughs for the new millennium.

---

[11] **glib**   casual and lighthearted

[12] **guinea pig**   small animal often used for experimentation

[13] **sorta (sort of) cool**   informal speech meaning really good

[14] **facial paralysis**   inability to move parts of their faces

[15] **pie in the sky**   something we can only dream about; not possible
now

[16] **bone graft**   repair that takes bone from one part of the body and
moves it to the damaged part

After You Read

Understanding the Text

A. True, False, or Impossible to Know? Read the statements below and write T (True), F (False), or I (Impossible to Know).

_____ **1.** Dr. Vacanti believes that he can build a human liver because it is a relatively simple organ.

_____ **2.** Of the 50,000 Americans who currently need new organs, approximately half will probably die before donors can be found.

_____ **3.** In Dr. Vacanti's opinion, using cells from the patient's body to grow new organs is better than transplanting organs from a donor.

_____ **4.** Hindu surgeons experimented with tissue replacement as early as the sixth century B.C.

_____ **5.** Most children born with Poland's syndrome die before they reach adulthood.

_____ **6.** Sean McCormack is the first human being in history with a tissue-engineered chest.

_____ **7.** Reconstructive surgery has allowed Sean to live a more or less normal life.

_____ **8.** Sean will never have problems with his chest again.

B. Consider the issues. Work with a partner to answer the questions below.

1. Read the second paragraph again. Why do you think the author mentions the monster created by Dr. Frankenstein (lines 4–7)? How is this related to Dr. Vacanti's opening statement?

2. Dr. Vacanti states that his professional goal is "to solve the problem of vital organ shortage" (line 14). Explain what he means by this. What has he done to work toward this goal?

3. In line 41, Dr. Vacanti comments that some people still think he is crazy. Why do they think so? Do you agree or disagree?

Inferencing

When you make an **inference,** you make a judgment based on the evidence. Readers often make inferences based on what the people included in a report say or do.

For example, from the first paragraph of the article on page 26, Dr. Vacanti speaks about building a human liver while collapsing in his chair. From this, we can infer that he is a very ambitious doctor who works very hard.

What can you infer about the people mentioned in the article? Read the evidence below, then circle the best answer.

1. Dr. Vacanti's eyes flash with energy as he talks about his dreams.

   a. he gets angry easily

   b. he is tired

   c. he is very enthusiastic

2. "My life never revolved around Poland's syndrome," Sean said.

   a. he mostly does whatever he wants to

   b. he has always been very careful

   c. he is upset about having the disease

3. It was often a torment for Sean's parents to watch him play baseball.

   a. They did not allow him to play because of his condition.

   b. They wanted him to live a more or less normal life.

   c. They hated baseball.

4. "Sorta cool," Sean says, smiling.

   a. He is pleased.

   b. He doesn't care.

   c. He is tired of it all.

5. In short, says his sister, Kelly "he's my 17-year-old brother who rides around town and does 17-year-old things."

   a. She is jealous of the attention her brother is getting.

   b. She is worried he will have an accident.

   c. She is very happy for her brother.

Using context to guess meaning

When you don't know the meaning of a word, look at the words around it to help you. You may be able to guess the meaning of the word from the surrounding context.

Complete the chart with information about the **boldfaced** words from the reading. First guess the meaning, then give a reason for your guess.

Example: ...the ghastly **monster** created by Dr. Frankenstein, with its translucent yellow skin, shriveled face, and black misshapen lips. (lines 5–7)

Meaning: a monster is an ugly, frightening creature

Reason: The words that follow describe such a creature.

1. Still in his **scrubs,** he has just come from the operating room... (lines 8–9)

Meaning: _____

Reason: _____

2. Instead of replacing a faltering organ with one **harvested** from someone else... (lines 17–18)

Meaning: _____

Reason: _____

3. ...Hindu surgeons began using arm skin to repair **mangled** noses. (lines 26–27)

Meaning: _____

Reason: _____

4. There is quite a difference between growing a relatively simple organ such as skin and growing a **complex** one like a liver. (lines 36–37)

Meaning: _____

Reason: _____

5. The cells would continue to grow inside his body, and as they did, the polymer disk would gradually **dissolve.** After three months, if everything went right, the disk would be completely gone... (lines 80–82)

Meaning: _____

Reason: _____

Modals of possibility
Could, may, or *might* + verb express the idea that something is possible or probable, but not certain.

It's beginning to look like it just *might work.*
(it is possible)

Passive forms of these verbs use *be* + past participle:

could
may   } be done
might

Both he and his parents were anxious to see what *could be done* about his condition.

A. Underline the verb phrases that express possibility in the sentences below. If the verb phrase is in the passive form, write a P at the end of the sentences.

1. Tissue regeneration could revolutionize the practice of medicine. _____

2. His parents worried that the baseball might kill him. _____

3. In the near future, injectable tissue may be used to repair damaged bones. _____

B. Rewrite the sentences in **A** above. If the main verb phrase is active, make it passive. If it is already passive, make it active. Make any other necessary changes.

1. *The practice of medicine could...* _____

_____

2. _____

_____

3. _____

_____

1. Imagine a future situation in which you or someone you know might benefit from Dr. Vacanti's research in tissue engineering. Explain what you think could happen.

2. **Group work.** What types of medical research are most important? Rank the following types of medical research in terms of their current importance (1 = the most important; 2; 3; etc.). Present your list to the class.

   _____   discovering a cure for AIDS

   _____   tissue engineering

   _____   prevention of heart disease

   _____   vital organ transplant

   _____   discovering a cure for cancer

   _____   discovering a cure for cholera

   _____   (other) _____

3. Choose one of the medical research areas from 2 above. Write a paragraph explaining (a) why this research is more important than all of the others and (b) what the results of the research could be in the next ten years.

Crossword Puzzle

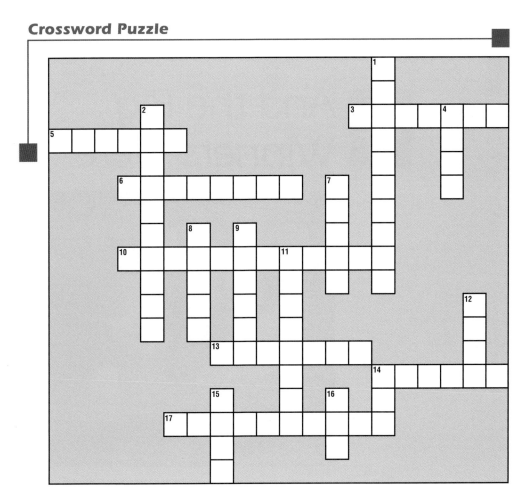

Use words from the reading to complete the crossword puzzle.

Across:

3 Badly damaged

5 Fix

6 A popular American sport

10 Fictional doctor who created a monster

13 Bone in the center of the chest

14 Special clothes worn in the operating room

17 Pharmacist or chemist

Down:

1 Move a living thing to a new place

2 The heart is one of these (2 words)

4 The batter hit a _____ drive.

7 A very important organ

8 Home of Hindu surgeons

9 Not accept

11 Sean was born with Poland's _____.

12 Casual and lighthearted

14 Pie in the _____

15 Slang for "really good"

16 A place for scientific research

Chapter ▲

4 And the Big Winners Were...

I'm very, very happy,
I'm very satisfied—
the dream is going on.

—Guus Hiddink
Soccer coach
(1946–   )

Chapter Focus

CONTENT:
Impact of World Cup soccer on players, fans, and host countries

READING SKILL:
Supporting main ideas

BUILDING VOCABULARY:
Using prefixes to determine meaning

LANGUAGE FOCUS:
Direct quotations

Before You Read

1. Look quickly over the newspaper article on pages 37–40 and read the title. What is "our game"? Why do you think it is the most popular game in the world?

2. The first paragraph of the reading mentions the "costs and the gains of World Cup 2002." What are some of the costs of hosting a major international event like the World Cup tournament? What are some of the gains?

3. This picture shows the Brazilian star Ronaldo just after his team scored a goal in the final match of World Cup 2002. In Brazil, the whole country began a week-long celebration. Why do athletes like Ronaldo get so much attention? Who are the most celebrated athletes in your country? How much do they get paid?

Reading Passage

AND THE BIG WINNERS WERE: RONALDO, SOUTH KOREA, AND "OUR GAME"

by Rob Hughes

from *The International Herald Tribune*

For the first time in World Cup history, the tournament was co-hosted by two Asian countries, Japan and South Korea. The South Korean team's thrilling win over Spain in overtime also marked the first time an Asian team had advanced to the semifinal round of the tournament.

1   Once the ball has stopped rolling, and the Brazilians stop partying, we can begin to count the costs and the gains of World Cup 2002.

It has been a tournament of many faces. Asia, first of all, was
5   unbroken ground,[1] a triumph of organization and security, and a lesson to the world in civility.[2]

---

[1] **unbroken ground**   a place where something has never been done before
[2] **civility**   courteous behavior; politeness

Brazil's team was bound for home, where the *Penca*—the historic fifth homecoming of the World Cup—will reignite[3] a population of 170 million whose problems with their beleaguered currency, the ***real***, will be set aside while the return of Ronaldo prolongs the **carnival**.[4]

10   He not only scores the goals, he finds the simple sentence that sums up a nation: "It's a fantastic feeling to be a Brazilian tonight," he said in Yokohama, Japan, as Sunday night turned into Monday morning.

Looking at him, Oliver Kahn, the beaten German goalkeeper and captain, could only say: "This is not about your club, it's about the
15   entire nation. When you look at the expectations and the enthusiasm of millions back home, you realize what's at stake."[5]

Maybe too much. Maybe **soccer** is exceeding its purpose in life and at this World Cup we have seen the best of it, and potentially the worst.

The skills of Brazil transcended everything,[6] and masked a little[7]
20   that this was a tournament of tired athletes (that's what they say, anyway, from France to Argentina, from England to Italy), and of uninspired, unpolished techniques.

But if Brazil was, without room for question, the champion, the Republic of Korea was a remarkable victor also. Its streets became
25   vast seas of red, impenetrable[8] lines of supporters like poppies in an overgrown field.

The celebrations that lasted from the first to the last ball that South Korea's sons chased were extraordinary. They were laced with fever,[9] and with the joyousness that Latin American countries parade[10] when
30   they win. There was something so proud, so deep, and so overwhelming[11] throughout South Korean society that with 5 million people in the town squares it still felt perfectly safe.

"We discovered unity in our people," said Chung Mong Joon, the man whose tigerish[12] fight within **FIFA** (Fédération Internationale de
35   Football Association), the governing body of world soccer, brought at least half a World Cup to his country.

---

[3] **reignite**   here, cause people to become happy again

[4] **prolongs the carnival**   makes the celebration last longer

[5] **what's at stake**   what can be won or lost

[6] **transcended everything**   were more important than all the problems

[7] **masked a little**   covered up somewhat

[8] **impenetrable**   tightly packed

[9] **laced with fever**   filled with excitement

[10] **parade**   show in a way that gets a lot of attention

[11] **overwhelming**   tremendous; overpowering

[12] **tigerish**   energetic; aggressive (like a tiger)

Speaking one morning at breakfast in Tokyo, Chung added: "They demonstrated they are free, they are mature, they are global citizens." And, he added, "nobody lost control." So, above all, the memory of
40 this World Cup is the people of South Korea. They have, as Chung says, discovered unity.

"The World Cup has been a lifetime experience," he said, "and even if in the end we were disappointed to lose the semifinal, I can say that I worked in FIFA for ten years without understanding the full impact
45 of the World Cup."

He knows it now. It was mounted at huge cost,[13] and in South Korea and Japan the infrastructure[14] will now have to be paid for. South Korea paid more than $2 billion to erect 10 new stadiums, while Japan's cost was close to twice as much.

50 We visitors—those not let down by the ticketing mess created by FIFA's appointed agency—were the beneficiaries.[15] There is no continent better served by state-of-the-art[16] stadiums than Asia now. How they will be used in the future (bearing in mind that a $660 million stadium costs at least $6 million a year in maintenance) is part
55 of the headache, the cost Asian taxpayers will bear.

There are, of course, some who are counting their profits, some bemoaning[17] losses from an event that claims to have been viewed by a cumulative audience of 42 billion over its 64 matches.

FIFA hopes that its television and marketing return nears $1
60 billion, and thus wipes out the bad blood[18] caused by its debts after one of its marketing companies collapsed[19] last year and its television group ran into financial problems this year.

But if soccer is inseparable from politics and commerce, the two sporting images that surpass all others are the awakening of South
65 Korea, and the heart-warming resurrection of Ronaldo.

It was as if 2002 was predestined[20] to be his tournament. He came back to rediscover himself, to conquer fear and long, long injuries, and inevitably, to score the two goals that defeated Germany in Yokohama on Sunday.

---

[13] **mounted at huge cost** very expensive to produce

[14] **infrastructure** buildings, roads, etc.

[15] **beneficiaries** people who receive the benefits

[16] **state-of-the-art** most modern; using the latest technology

[17] **bemoaning** regretting; feeling sorry about

[18] **bad blood** negative feelings; anger

[19] **collapsed** failed; went out of business

[20] **predestined** fated; decided in advance

70   Magnificent. Ronaldo is a young man, still only 25, who has so much wealth that he did not need to push his body through pain. He could have retired on his fame. But in his soul is to be a footballer, and every Brazilian aspires to winning the World Cup.

Long may he thrill us.

75   South Korea and Japan did not manage to smooth over[21] their separate customs (either at the airports or at the heart of a joint tournament). They remain suspicious and often incompatible neighbors. But both saw in the flesh[22] the greatest teams and the greatest player of this World Cup.

80   Yet football crossed the boundaries. North Koreans peeped[23] at the games, which is an improvement on 1988, when Pyongyang remained a closed and shuttered window, ignoring the world at play.

The hope is that, long after the stadiums are closed, some of them becoming relics[24] even in their imaginative structural design, the
85   human sharing of this event will remain with those who hosted it.

A boundary has been crossed, and FIFA now talks, optimistically, of Africa in 2010 (after Germany in 2006).

If one person found the joy in this now gargantuan[25] business enterprise, then soccer, the game, is still a remarkable life force.[26]
90   And I know of one. Po Soon Bun is 68, and a grandmother.

"I did not watch football, even on television, before this World Cup," she said. "I could not understand those boys running after the ball. But now, I read every World Cup article in the newspapers. It's amazing what football can do to you." Welcome to our game,
95   Madame. You are never too young or too old to catch the fever.[27]

About the **Source**

The *International Herald Tribune* is a daily English-language newspaper with a worldwide circulation. With head editorial offices in France, the *IHT* publishes international political, business, and sports news.

---

[21] **smooth over**   make more similar or compatible
[22] **in the flesh**   in person
[23] **peeped**   took a look
[24] **relics**   things that remain after a long time has passed
[25] **gargantuan**   huge
[26] **life force**   motivation to live happily; source of joy
[27] **catch the fever**   get excited about something (along with a lot of other people)

After You Read

Understanding the Text

A. Multiple choice. For each item below, circle the best answer.

1. This article was written _____.

   a. just before the final match between Brazil and Germany

   b. a year after the teams had returned home

   c. shortly after the tournament was over

   d. after all the debts for hosting the tournament had been paid

2. The author makes all of the following points except _____.

   a. Ronaldo is a great player, both physically and mentally

   b. the German fans were remarkably civil

   c. the whole world was impressed by the South Korean fans

   d. soccer has the power to bring joy to the lives of ordinary people

3. Ronaldo's success was especially heartwarming because _____.

   a. he is Brazilian

   b. it made him richer

   c. he had recovered from serious injuries

   d. he will retire soon

4. Which of the following does the author give as an example of a "boundary" being crossed?

   a. Korea and Japan became friendlier toward each other.

   b. North Korea did not ignore the games.

   c. The Korean coach was from Europe.

   d. The South Korean team made it to the semifinals.

5. The new stadiums built for the event are examples of the _____ a country must have to put on a big international sporting event.

   a. full impact

   b. communications

   c. beneficiaries

   d. infrastructure

6. Which of these statements do you think the author would agree with most?

   a. World Cup 2002 was expensive but well worth it.

   b. People around the world pay too much attention to football.

   c. Professional soccer players make more money than they should.

   d. The only winners at World Cup 2002 were the Brazilians.

B. Consider the issues. *Work with a partner to answer the questions below.*

   1. Find the quotations below in the text. For each quotation, fill in the speaker's name and explain briefly who the person is.

QUOTATION	SPEAKER	DESCRIPTION
a. "It's a fantastic feeling to be a Brazilian tonight."	Ronaldo	Brazilian soccer star
b. "This is not about your club, it's about the entire nation."		
c. "The World Cup has been a lifetime experience."		
d. "I could not understand those boys running after the ball."		

   Why do you think the author included these quotations in the article?

   2. In lines 4–41, the author praises Asia for giving the world "a lesson in civility." Explain in your own words what this means and give at least one example.

Supporting main ideas

Writers usually focus on a few main ideas in a piece of writing. They use related ideas as well as interesting details and examples to support these main points. **Supporting ideas, details,** and **examples** help the reader to understand and appreciate the writer's main ideas.

Examples:

South Korea and Japan were extremely successful as host nations for World Cup 2002. **(main idea)**

The tournament was well organized. **(related idea)**

Both countries built state-of-the-art stadiums. **(supporting detail)**

Even with 5 million people in the town squares it still felt perfectly safe. **(supporting example)**

A. Look back at the reading and find at least three related ideas, details, or examples that support each of the main ideas below.

MAIN IDEA
The skills of the Brazilian team transcended everything.

SUPPORTING INFORMATION
1. _____
2. _____
3. _____

MAIN IDEA
Football is a remarkable life force.

SUPPORTING INFORMATION
1. _____
2. _____
3. _____

B. Identify at least one more of the writer's main ideas. What related ideas, details, and/or examples does he use to support it?

MAIN IDEA	
	1. _____
	2. _____

Using prefixes to determine meaning

Prefixes like *re-*, *un-*, and *inter-* can be combined with some words to change their meaning.

re + discover = rediscover (discover again)

inter + national = international (between or among nations)

Prefixes are always attached to the beginning of words. Understanding common prefixes can help you figure out the meanings of unknown words.

A. Look back at the reading and find examples of words that begin with the following prefixes. Explain the meaning of each example.

PREFIX	EXAMPLE	MEANING
1. re- (again)	reignite	become happy again
2. un- (not)		
3. im- (not)		
4. over- (more than usual)		
5. extra- (beyond)		
6. semi- (half or one of two)		
7. in- (not)		
8. pre- (before)		

B. Complete each sentence with a word from the box.

immature	reconsider	overtime	precaution	unbeaten

1. As an extra security _____, police inspected the bags of all ticket holders at the gates.

2. The German team was _____ until the final match.

3. South Korea won its match against Spain in _____.

4. The behavior of the Asian fans was considered remarkably civil because in other parts of the world, the behavior of soccer fans is often _____.

5. Both the 1988 Olympics and World Cup 2002 have caused the world to _____ its perception of Asia.

Direct quotations

A **direct quotation** reports something that someone said. Quotation marks " " indicate that the words inside are exactly as they were spoken. The speaker may be identified at the beginning, in the middle, or at the end of the quotation.

Examples:

Oliver Kahn, the beaten German goalkeeper and captain, could only say: "This is not about your club, it's about the entire nation."

"We discovered unity in our people," said Chung Mong Joon.

The World Cup has been a lifetime experience," he said, "and even if in the end we were disappointed to lose the semifinal, I can say that I worked in FIFA for ten years without understanding the full impact of the World Cup."

When reporters interview people, they ask direct questions and write down the exact words people say. They use these direct quotations to support their main ideas and to make their articles more lively and convincing.

A. Read the last two paragraphs of the article again (page 40). Then, without looking back, put quotation marks around the sentences that were spoken directly by Po Soon Bun.

Po Soon Bun is 68, and a grandmother.

I could not understand those boys running after the ball.

Welcome to our game, Madame.

But now, I read every World Cup article in the newspapers.

B. Look back at the direct quotation from Ronaldo (line 11) and answer the following questions.

1. What were Ronaldo's exact words?

_____

2. What question do you think he was answering?

_____

3. Why do you think the reporter (Rob Hughes) decided to include this quotation in the article?

_____

1. Although the costs are great and there are a lot of problems to solve, many countries compete fiercely for the opportunity to host a major international sporting event, such as the World Cup or the **Olympics**. Why do you think this is so?

2. **Group work.** Imagine that your group has been appointed to decide whether or not the next World Cup (or other big sporting event) should be held in your hometown or city. Give the event a name and a year. Then make two lists, (1) the potential benefits the event could bring and (2) the potential problems it could cause.

BENEFITS	PROBLEMS
watching great athletes	security

3. As a group, discuss both the benefits and the problems. Decide whether you are FOR or AGAINST hosting the event. Based on your decision, write a proposal in favor of or opposed to the whole idea.

   a. Make a general statement explaining your group's decision.

   b. Use ideas, details, and/or examples from your discussion to support your main point.

   c. Appoint a spokesperson from your group to read your proposal to the class and answer questions.

Crossword Puzzle

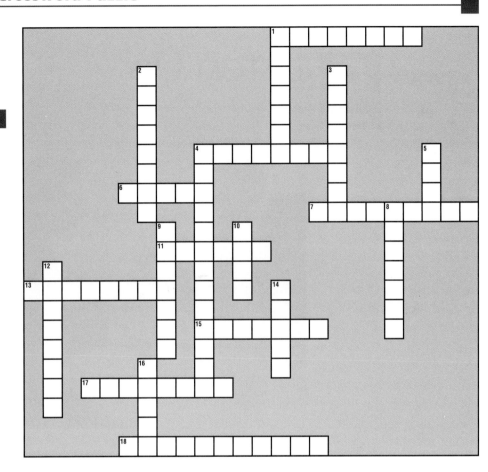

Use words from the reading to complete the crossword puzzle.

Across:

1 Asian fans taught the world a lesson in _____.
4 Very negative feelings (two words)
6 One of the host countries in 2002
7 Capital of North Korea
11 First name of the German goalkeeper
13 One of the most famous sporting events in the world (two words)
15 Brazilian superstar
17 Like a tiger
18 Decided in advance

Down:

1 Nobody lost _____.
2 A huge celebration
3 A _____ has been crossed.
4 People who receive the benefits
5 Governing body of world soccer (acronym)
8 Host country for World Cup 2006
9 Bright red flowers
10 Unit of currency in Brazil
12 Large Japanese city
14 A very, very old thing
16 It's never to late to catch the _____.

Chapter Listen Up

We have two ears and one mouth so that we can listen twice as much as we speak.

—*Epictetus*
Philosopher and teacher
(A.D. 55–138)

Chapter Focus

CONTENT:
Becoming an effective listener

READING SKILL:
Recognizing sentence transitions

BUILDING VOCABULARY:
Using adverbs and intensifiers

LANGUAGE FOCUS:
Using punctuation: dashes, colons, and semicolons

Before You Read

1. What are the qualities of a good listener? Brainstorm with your class. Make a list of as many descriptive words and phrases as you can.

2. In the introduction to the reading (pages 49–50), the author presents a short workplace conversation between a supervisor (Dave) and an employee (Bill). Take a quick look at the conversation. Is there anything that surprises you? What do you think it is an example of?

3. What do you think is going on in this cartoon? What do you think may have led to this situation?

"Remember when I said I was going to be honest with you, Jeff? That was a big, fat lie."

Reading Passage

LISTEN UP

by Madelyn Burley-Allen

from *Human Resource Magazine*

1   Imagine the following supervisor-employee exchange at your workplace:

Bill (employee):   **Dave**, I'm really discouraged about the way things have been going[1] on the job. It just never
5   goes the way I expect it to. And, it seems like you're never around[2] anymore.

Dave (supervisor): Sounds as though you've been doing quite a bit of thinking about this. Go ahead.

---

[1] **the way things have been going**   recent events

[2] **you're never around**   you are not here

| 10 | Bill: | Well, we are a week behind in production, and our supplies are not coming in on time. I feel swamped[3] and unable to catch up. And, when I have tried to find you lately to see about getting some extra help down there, you are not available. |

Dave: Seems that you feel cut off from any support from me.

You have just read an example of good listening. Listening is probably the most essential component of being a successful supervisor. The one attribute most often stated about a well-liked boss is, "he or she really listens to me." As Dave illustrated in the above brief scenario, he was on his way to clearing up a misunderstanding, building rapport,[4] developing respect and establishing a feeling of cooperation.

Dave was establishing **a caring and understanding environment** with Bill. He did this by having the attitude about people that included the following values:

- "I'm responsible for my actions, feelings and behavior."

- "I don't have the power to change others, only myself."

- "Refraining from judging others will assist me in listening to them effectively."

- "I allow others to be on an equal level with myself."

These values influence Dave to listen empathetically,[5] communicate openly, describe behavior nonjudgmentally,[6] and assume responsibility for his feelings and behavior, and, in turn, this enhances the self-esteem of people around him.

Listening Is a Skill

Effective listening is a learned skill; it doesn't happen automatically for most people. In addition, there are few rewards for listening, but there are punishments for not listening. How do you feel when listeners are not paying attention to you by looking at their watches, doing some activity or not acknowledging what you've said? You probably felt put down[7] or, even worse, you felt like you were talking to a wall. Listeners have a lot more power and impact on the talker than most people realize.

---

[3] **I feel swamped**   I have too much work; I am overwhelmed

[4] **building rapport**   establishing a good working relationship

[5] **listen empathetically**   listen in a way that shows understanding of a person's situation and feelings

[6] **nonjudgmentally**   openly; without having an opinion beforehand

[7] **put down**   insulted

In addition, many people tend to assume[8] listening is basically the same as hearing—a dangerous misconception that leads to believing that effective listening is instinctive. As a result, supervisors make little effort to develop listening skills and unknowingly neglect a vital communication function. Research shows that the average person on the job spends 40 percent of his time listening, 35 percent talking, 16 percent reading, and 9 percent writing.

On average, people only are about 35 percent efficient as listeners. This lack of effective listening often results in missed opportunities to avoid misunderstandings, conflict, poor decision-making or a crisis because a problem wasn't identified in time.

Three Levels of Listening

Awareness of your listening behavior will go a long way in helping you become an effective listener. Listening can be divided into three levels, which are characterized by certain behaviors that affect listening efficiency.

Most often, people have difficulty listening effectively when in a conflict situation, when dealing with emotional people, when having criticism directed at them, when being disciplined or when feeling anxious, fearful or angry.

The following descriptions of the three levels will help you understand the distinction between how each level is expressed:

Level 1. A person at Level 1 demonstrates the characteristics of a good listener. These listeners look for an area of interest in the talker's message; they view it as an opportunity to gather new and useful information. Effective listeners are aware of their personal biases,[9] are better able to avoid making automatic judgments about the talker and to avoid being influenced by **emotionally charged words**.[10] Good listeners suspend judgment and are empathetic to the other person's feelings. They can see things from the other person's point of view and inquire about rather than advocate a position.

Level 1 listeners use extra thought time to anticipate the talker's next statement, to mentally summarize the stated message, evaluate what was said, and to consciously notice nonverbal cues.[11] Their overall focus is to listen with understanding and respect. In the example at the beginning of this article, Dave did an excellent job responding to Bill at Level 1. Read the brief scenario again with the

---

[8] **tend to assume**   are inclined to think that

[9] **personal biases**   their own views and opinions

[10] **emotionally charged words**   words that make people feel upset

[11] **nonverbal cues**   ways people communicate in addition to words, for example, eye movement, gestures, tone of voice, etc.

80   description of Level 1 in mind and you will see how Dave illustrates these characteristics.

    Level 2. At this level, a person is mainly listening to words and the content of what is being said, but does not fully understand what the words mean. This results in the semantic barrier[12]—the meaning of
85   words. There are thousands of words in the English vocabulary. The average adult in the United States uses 500 of these words most often. However, each one of these words has between 20 and 25 meanings. This means that we are using 500 words with the possibility of 12,500 different meanings. Adding to the confusion is
90   the **variety of slang**[13] Americans use, double meanings of many words, and on and on.

    The important factor in all of this is that words don't communicate. It's the meaning and the understanding of words that make communication work. For instance, Level 2 listeners are zeroing in
95   on[14] words, but many times, they miss the intent, such as what is being expressed nonverbally through tone of voice, body posture, etc.

    As a result, Level 2 listeners hear what the speaker says but make little effort to understand the speaker's intent. Needless to say, this can lead to misunderstanding, and a variety of negative feelings. In
100 addition, since the listener appears to be listening by nodding his head in agreement and not asking clarifying questions,[15] the talker may be lulled into a false sense of being understood.

    Level 3. At this level, people are tuning out the speaker, daydreaming, or faking attention[16] while thinking about unrelated
105 matters. This causes relationship breakdowns, conflicts and poor decision making because the person is busy finding fault, responding defensively, or becoming overly emotional. All of this influences either the talker or the listener to move into the flight-or-fight mode.[17]

    As you examine these three levels, you can imagine how different
110 groups and individuals would work together based on which level they are activating.

---

[12] **semantic barrier**   breakdown in communication based on the meaning of words

[13] **slang**   very casual language used by a particular group, often containing many newly invented terms

[14] **zeroing in on**   focusing on

[15] **clarifying questions**   questions that help the listener understand what the speaker is saying

[16] **faking attention**   pretending to listen

[17] **flight-or-fight mode**   responding by walking away angrily or arguing

Benefits of Level 1 Listening

There are many benefits for supervisors who listen effectively at Level
1. When employees know they are talking to a listener instead of a
115 supervisor who sits in judgment, they openly suggest ideas and share
feelings. When this happens the two of them can work as a team
creatively solving the problem instead of placing blame on each other.

As an effective listener, you set in motion a positive, mutually
rewarding process by demonstrating interest in the employee and
120 what he or she is saying. This empathetic listening encourages
honesty, mutual respect, understanding, and a feeling of security in
the employee.

Listening also encourages employees to feel self-confident. This in
turn can build their self-esteem and a feeling of being empowered.

125 Guidelines for Empathetic Listening

- Be attentive. You will create a positive atmosphere through your
  nonverbal behavior, for instance, eye contact, an open relaxed
  posture, a friendly facial expression and a pleasant tone of voice.
  When you are alert, attentive and relaxed, the other person feels
130 important and more secure.

- Be interested in the speaker's needs. Remember listening at
  Level 1 means you listen with understanding and mutual respect.

- Listen from a caring attitude. Be a sounding board by allowing
  the speaker to bounce ideas and feelings off of you.[18] Don't ask a
135 lot of questions right away. Questions can often come across as
  if the person is being "grilled."[19]

- Act like a mirror. Reflect back what you think the other person is
  feeling. Summarize what the person said to make sure you
  understand what he's saying.

140 - Don't let the other person "hook you." This can happen when
  you get personally involved. Getting personally involved in a
  problem usually results in anger and hurt feelings or motivates
  you to jump to conclusions and be judgmental.

- Use verbal cues. Acknowledge the person's statement using brief
145 expressions such as, "uh-huh," "I see," or "interesting."
  Encourage the speaker to reveal more by saying "tell me about
  it," "let's discuss it," or "I'd be interested in what you have to say."

---

[18] **bounce ideas off of you**   make suggestions freely and receive helpful
feedback

[19] **grilled**   (slang) made to feel uncomfortable by being asked a series of
tough questions

Following these guidelines will help you be a successful listener. It's critical to create the habit of being a Level 1 listener by applying 150 these guidelines on a daily basis so that they are internalized as part of your listening behavior. You can do this by taking time each day to carry out these skills successfully in a specific situation. You will be surprised at the results.

About the Author

Madelyn Burley-Allen founded Dynamics of Human Behavior in 1972. She has given more than 2,000 seminars in the United States, China, India, Russia, Singapore, Indonesia, and Malaysia. She has published several books, including *Listening: The Forgotten Skill*.

After You Read

Understanding the Text

A. True or False? Read the statements below and write T (True) or F (False).

_____ **1.** The author's purpose is to help people become better listeners.

_____ **2.** According to the author, listening is one of the most important skills a person needs to be a good supervisor.

_____ **3.** The opening conversation between Bill and Dave is intended to give readers an example of poor communication on the job.

_____ **4.** The article states that good listening skills come naturally to most people.

_____ **5.** In the author's breakdown of listening efficiency, Level 1 is the most effective and Level 3 is the least effective.

_____ **6.** The author has observed that most people do not listen to everyone at the same level of efficiency.

_____ **7.** The fact that most English words have many meanings supports the idea that people do not communicate with words alone.

B. Label descriptive features. Read each statement and identify it as a description of a Level 1, Level 2, or Level 3 listener.

_____1_____ **1.** Looks for an area of interest in the talker's message.

_____ **2.** Pretends to listen but is really thinking about something else.

_____ **3.** Listens mainly to words but does not really try to understand what the speaker is getting at.

_____ **4.** Responds defensively or becomes overly emotional.

_____ **5.** Listens with both understanding and respect.

C. Consider the issues. Work with a partner to answer the questions below.

1. Read the conversation on pages 49–50 aloud with your partner. What level of listening does this exchange illustrate? Explain how.

2. Check (√) if you agree or disagree with each of the values stated in the chart below. Then explain why.

a. I am responsible for my own actions, feelings, and behaviors.
☐ Agree   Why? _____
☐ Disagree _____

b. I don't have the power to change others, only myself.
☐ Agree   Why? _____
☐ Disagree _____

c. Refraining from judging others will assist me in listening to them effectively.
☐ Agree   Why? _____
☐ Disagree _____

d. I allow others to be on an equal level with myself.
☐ Agree   Why? _____
☐ Disagree _____

3. Based on the article, would you consider yourself mainly a Level 1, 2, or 3 listener? Why?

Recognizing sentence transitions

Sentence transitions are words and phrases that build bridges between sentences so that readers can stay on track. One way of making a sentence transition is to repeat the same word (or a word with almost the same meaning) as in the previous sentence.

> You have just read an example of good *listening. Listening* is probably the most essential component of being a successful supervisor.

Another way is to use a pronoun to refer to a word or phrase in the previous sentence:

> *Good listeners* suspend judgment and are empathetic to the other person's feelings. *They* can see things from the other person's point of view.

A third way is to use a connecting word or phrase, such as *however, on the other hand, for example, as a result, needless to say, in addition,* or *therefore.*

> Effective listening is a learned skill; it doesn't happen automatically for most people. *In addition,* there are few rewards for listening, but there are punishments for not listening.

A. Read each pair of sentences from the reading and underline the words or phrases that connect them. There may be more than one pair of connecting words or phrases in each set.

1. Dave was establishing a caring and understanding environment with Bill. He did this by having the attitude about people that included the following values.

2. On average, people only are about 35 percent efficient as listeners. This lack of effective listening often results in missed opportunities.

3. Don't let the other person "hook you." This can happen when you get personally involved.

4. There are thousands of words in the English vocabulary. The average adult in the United States uses 500 of these words most often.

5. Take a moment to think back to your experiences when working with different individuals and groups. What made the experience positive?

B. Read the following pairs of sentences from the article. Complete the sentences using connecting words or phrases from the box (you will only need three).

in addition	as a result	however	for instance
therefore	needless to say	on the other hand	

1. Listeners have a lot more power and impact on the talker than most people realize. _____, many people tend to assume listening is basically the same as hearing—a dangerous misconception that leads to believing that effective listening is instinctive.

2. The average adult in the United States uses 500 of these words most often. _____, each one of these words has between 20 and 25 meanings.

3. It's the meaning and the understanding of words that make communication work. _____, Level 2 listeners are zeroing in on words, but many times, they miss the intent, such as what is being expressed nonverbally through tone of voice, body posture, etc.

> ### Using adverbs and intensifiers
> **Adverbs of manner** usually follow a verb. These words usually end in -*ly* and tell how or in what way something is done, happens, or is true.
>
> These values influence Dave to listen *empathetically*, communicate *openly*, and describe behavior *nonjudgmentally*.
>
> An **intensifier** signals to what degree something is true. Intensifiers can modify adjectives or adverbs.
>
> I'm *really* discouraged. (How discouraged are you?)
>
> He was speaking *too* fast for me to understand. (How fast...?)
>
> Other words used as intensifiers include *very, quite, totally, seriously, absolutely, partly, somewhat, moderately, extremely.*

A. Complete the following statements using as many adverbs as you can think of. Refer back to the article if you need inspiration.

1. A good supervisor listens

2. An effective communicator speaks

B. Read the conversation below and underline the intensifiers.

Joe (employee): Jane, I'm totally discouraged about the way things have been going on the job. It never goes the way I expect it to. And, it seems like you're almost never around anymore.

Jane (supervisor): That's completely ridiculous! You're imagining things. I'm the very first to get here in the morning and the very last to leave at night. Who told you that you have the right to criticize the boss? If you're not extremely careful, you could get fired.

Using punctuation: dashes, colons, and semicolons
Writers use **dashes** (—) to separate parts of sentences that add extra information or say the same thing in another way. In spoken language, a pause has the same function as a dash.

This results in the semantic barrier—the meaning of words.

A **colon** (:) is used to call attention to the words that follow it. For example, a colon often introduces a list of similar items.

Good speakers make use of several modes of nonverbal communication: tone of voice, body posture, gestures, facial expression, and eye movement.

A **semicolon** (;) connects two closely related parts of a sentence. Each part must have its own subject and verb.

Effective listening is a learned skill; it doesn't happen automatically for most people.

When used in this way, the semicolon replaces a connecting word such as *and, but, or, for, so, yet.*

In each of the following sentences, add the missing punctuation (dash, colon, semicolon).

1. Many people tend to assume listening is basically the same as hearing—a dangerous misconception that leads to believing that effective listening is instinctive.

2. These levels are not sharply distinct but rather general categories into which people fall they may overlap or interchange, depending on what is happening.

3. As a person moves from Level 3 the least effective to Level 1 the most effective the potential for understanding and retention of what is said and for effective communication increases.

4. This depends on several things the circumstances, their attitudes about the other person, and past experience.

Discussion & Writing

1. After reading the article, do you think you will change the way you listen to people? In what ways? Would you recommend the article to anyone else you know? Why or why not?

2. Work with a partner. Imagine that you are both participating in a seminar to help employees and supervisors improve their listening skills.

    a. Decide who will be the supervisor and who will be the employee. Read the conversation on pages 49–50 aloud. Then switch roles and read it again. Discuss how you felt playing each role.

    b. Write a scene of your own that illustrates Level 2 or Level 3 listening. Practice reading your dialogue aloud, including appropriate nonverbal cues like facial expressions and gestures. Then act out your scene for the class.

3. Have you ever had a problem communicating? Think of a time when you had a problem and you tried unsuccessfully to explain it to someone. You felt like you were talking to a wall. Write a letter to a friend, explaining what happened and how you felt.

Crossword Puzzle

Use words from the reading to complete the crossword puzzle.

Across:

1 To speak out in support of

2 The way you hold your body

4 _____ can be helpful if it offers thoughtful ideas for improvement.

8 A strong personal opinion

11 A natural guess about something

13 To be mistaken

15 Try not to _____ when someone is talking to you.

17 To give someone a feeling of confidence

18 Show or act out

Down:

1 To think ahead

3 The substance of a communication

5 A good listener can have a strong _____ on the speaker.

6 To make something better

7 _____ of voice

9 To ask a question

10 One small part of a drama

12 To feel what another person feels is to have _____.

14 Mutual respect is important to good _____ in the workplace.

16 To express your inner thoughts and feelings

Chapter 6

Don't Let Stereotypes Warp Your Judgment

A person is a person because he recognizes others as persons.

—Archbishop Desmond Tutu
Religious leader
(1931–)

Chapter Focus

CONTENT:
Harmful effects of stereotyping

READING SKILL:
Recognizing sources

BUILDING VOCABULARY:
Using verbs as adjectives

LANGUAGE FOCUS:
Using relative clauses with *who*, *which*, or *that*

Before You Read

1. Describe the person in the photograph on page 62. Where do you think she lives? What does she do for a living? What do you think of her appearance? Give reasons for your answers.

2. A stereotype is a very simple, standard generalization held by one group of people about another group. Stereotypes are often based on gender, age, nationality, race, or profession. In the chart below, list some adjectives that come to mind when you think about each group.

GROUP	STEREOTYPICAL DESCRIPTION
French men	
Chinese doctors	
American teenagers	
Elderly professors	

Can you think of some ways in which stereotyping these groups of people could be harmful?

3. Read the first two paragraphs of the article. Why do you think the author asks these questions? What is he trying to get the reader to think about?

Reading Passage

DON'T LET STEREOTYPES WARP[1] YOUR JUDGMENT

by Robert Heilbroner

from *Think Magazine*

1   Is a girl called Gloria apt to be better looking than one called Bertha? Are criminals more likely to be dark than blond? Can you tell a good deal about someone's personality from hearing his voice briefly over the phone? Can a person's nationality be pretty 5 accurately guessed from his photograph? Does the fact that someone wears glasses imply that he is intelligent?

The answer to all these questions is obviously, "No."

---

[1] **warp**   bend or twist; influence in a negative way

Yet, from all the evidence at hand, most of us believe these things. Ask any college boy if he'd rather take his chances with a
10 Gloria or a Bertha, or ask a college girl if she'd rather blind-date[2] a Richard or a Cuthbert. In fact, you don't have to ask: college students in questionnaires have revealed that names conjure up the same images in their minds as they do in yours—and for as little reason.

Look into the favorite suspects of persons who report "suspicious
15 characters" and you will find a large percentage of them to be "swarthy"[3] or "dark and foreign-looking"—despite the testimony[4] of criminologists that criminals do not tend to be dark, foreign, or "wild-eyed." Delve into the main asset[5] of a telephone stock swindler[6] and you will find it to be a marvelously confidence-inspiring telephone
20 "personality." And whereas we all think we know what an Italian or a Swede looks like, it is the sad fact that when a group of **Nebraska** students sought to match faces and nationalities of 15 European countries, they were scored wrong in 93 percent of their identifications. Finally, for all the fact that[7] horn-rimmed glasses[8]
25 have now become the standard television sign of an "intellectual," optometrists know that the main thing that distinguishes people with glasses is just bad eyes.

Stereotypes are a kind of gossip about the world, a gossip that makes us pre-judge people before we ever lay eyes on them. Hence it
30 is not surprising that stereotypes have something to do with the dark world of prejudice. Explore most prejudices (note that the word means prejudgment) and you will find a cruel stereotype at the core of each one.

Why is it that we stereotype the world in such irrational and
35 harmful fashion? In part, we begin to typecast people in our childhood years. Early in life, as every parent whose child has watched a **TV Western** knows, we learn to spot the Good Guys from the Bad Guys. Some years ago, a social psychologist showed very clearly how powerful these stereotypes of childhood vision are. He
40 secretly asked the most popular youngsters in an elementary school to make errors in their morning gym exercises. Afterward, he asked

---

[2] **blind-date**   go out on a date with someone you haven't met before

[3] **swarthy**   having dark skin and hair

[4] **testimony**   statements that support a claim

[5] **delve into the main asset**   find out the most useful skill

[6] **telephone stock swindler**   criminal who sells fake stocks over the telephone

[7] **for all the fact that**   even though

[8] **horn-rimmed glasses**   glasses with frames made of thick, dark-colored plastic

the class if anyone had noticed any mistakes during gym period. Oh, yes, said the children. But it was the *unpopular* members of the class—the "bad guys"—they remembered as being out of step.

45   We not only grow up with standardized pictures forming inside of us, but as grown-ups we are constantly having them thrust upon us. Some of them, like the half-joking, half-serious stereotypes of mothers-in-law, or country yokels,[9] or psychiatrists, are dinned into us[10] by the stock jokes we hear and repeat. In fact, without such
50   stereotypes, there would be a lot fewer jokes. Still other stereotypes are perpetuated by the advertisements we read, the movies we see, the books we read.

And finally, we tend to stereotype because it helps us make sense out of a highly confusing world, a world which **William James** once
55   described as "one great, blooming, buzzing confusion." It is a curious fact that if we don't *know* what we're looking at, we are often quite literally[11] unable to *see* what we're looking at. People who recover their sight after a lifetime of blindness actually cannot at first tell a triangle from a square. A visitor to a factory sees only noisy chaos
60   where the superintendent sees a perfectly synchronized[12] flow of work. As **Walter Lippmann** has said, "For the most part we do not first see, and then define; we define first, and then we see."

Stereotypes are one way in which we "define" the world in order to see it. They classify the infinite variety of human beings into a
65   convenient handful of "types" toward whom we learn to act in stereotyped fashion. Life would be a wearing process if we had to start from scratch[13] with each and every human contact. Stereotypes economize on our mental effort by covering up the blooming, buzzing confusion with big recognizable cut-outs.[14] They save us the "trouble"
70   of finding out what the world is like—they give it its accustomed look.

Thus the trouble is that stereotypes make us mentally lazy. As **S.I. Hayakawa**, the authority on semantics, has written: "the danger of stereotypes lies not in their existence, but in the fact that they become for all people some of the time, and for some people all of the
75   time, *substitutes for observation.*"

---

[9] **country yokels** people who live in rural areas, especially those without sophisticated manners

[10] **dinned into us** fixed in our minds

[11] **quite literally** in fact; actually

[12] **perfectly synchronized** smoothly coordinated

[13] **start from scratch** begin all over again

[14] **big, recognizable cut-outs** large paper shapes of people made of stiff paper or cardboard

Hence, quite aside from the injustice which stereotypes do to others, they impoverish ourselves. A person who lumps the world into simple categories, who type-casts all labor leaders as "racketeers,"[15] all businessmen as "reactionaries,"[16] all Harvard men as "snobs," and all Frenchmen as "sexy," is in danger of becoming a stereotype himself. He loses his capacity to be himself—which is to say, to see the world in his own absolutely unique, inimitable,[17] and independent fashion.

Impoverishing as they are, stereotypes are not easy to get rid of. The world we type-cast may be no better than a Grade B movie,[18] but at least we know what to expect of our stock characters. When we let them act for themselves in the strangely unpredictable way that people do act, who knows but that many of our fondest convictions will be proved wrong?

Nor do we suddenly drop our standardized pictures for a blinding vision of the Truth. Sharp swings of ideas about people often just substitute one stereotype for another. The true process of change is a slow one that adds bits and pieces of reality to the pictures in our heads, until gradually they take on some of the blurriness of life itself.

Can we speed the process along? Of course we can.

First, we can become *aware* of the standardized pictures in our heads, in other peoples' heads, in the world around us.

Second, we can become suspicious of all judgments that we allow exceptions to "prove." There is no more chastening thought[19] than that in the vast intellectual adventure of science, it takes but one tiny exception to topple a whole edifice of ideas.[20]

Third, we can learn to be wary of generalizations about people. As F. Scott Fitzgerald once wrote: "Begin with an individual, and before you know it you have created a type; begin with a type, and you find you have created nothing."

Most of the time, when we type-cast the world, we are not in fact generalizing about people at all. We are only revealing the embarrassing facts about the pictures that hang in the gallery of stereotypes in our own heads.

---

[15] **racketeer**   person who makes money illegally; a type of criminal

[16] **reactionaries**   people who oppose change; extremely conservative people

[17] **inimitable**   impossible to imitate; one of a kind

[18] **grade B movie**   a second-rate film

[19] **chastening thought**   a realization that makes one more humble or restrained

[20] **topple a whole edifice of ideas**   disprove an entire system of thought

After You Read

Understanding the Text

A. Multiple choice. For each item below, circle the best answer.

1. The purpose of the questions in the first paragraph is to _____.
   a. analyze some common stereotypes
   b. cause readers to think about some common stereotypes
   c. get information from readers about their stereotypes
   d. make readers laugh at themselves

2. According to the author, the names "Bertha" and "Cuthbert" are _____.
   a. less appealing than names like Gloria and Richard
   b. more appealing than names like Gloria and Richard
   c. very popular among college students
   d. not an important factor in determining a person's image

3. From the testimony of criminologists, we can conclude that _____.
   a. most suspicious characters have dark complexions
   b. telephone swindlers have attractive personalities
   c. there is no connection between criminal activity and skin color
   d. criminals look very different from ordinary people

4. According to the author, many people believe that wearing glasses is a sign of _____.
   a. a person's nationality
   b. the dark world of prejudice
   c. watching too much television
   d. intellectual ability

5. Stereotypes are at the core of all of the following except _____.

    a. the way we tend to prejudge people

    b. the way we think about ourselves

    c. our efforts to make sense of the world

    d. the ability to see ourselves as unique

6. In general, media such as movies, television shows, and advertisements have the effect of _____.

    a. getting rid of stereotypes

    b. forming and strengthening stereotypes

    c. helping youngsters distinguish between good and bad

    d. helping youngsters recognize their mistakes

7. From S.I. Hayakawa's statement about stereotypes (lines 72–75), he would probably agree that _____.

    a. stereotypes are more harmful than they are helpful

    b. there is no harm in jokes based on stereotypes

    c. most intellectuals wear horn-rimmed glasses

    d. stereotypes are more helpful than they are harmful

B. Consider the issues. Work with a partner to answer the questions below.

1. The author of this article describes several stereotypes held by many Americans. List three additional examples in the chart below. On the right side of the chart, describe a stereotype held by people in your country about the same group.

GROUP	STEREOTYPE HELD BY AMERICANS	STEREOTYPE HELD BY _____
criminals	_swarthy_	

2. Choose one example of a stereotype held by many people in your country. How do you think this stereotype was formed? Can you think of any exceptions?

3. Do you agree with the author that stereotypes can be harmful? Why or why not? Give at least one example to support your opinion.

Recognizing sources

Writers often refer to other sources of information on a subject in order to support their main points. These sources may include other writers, research reports, or surveys.

When a group of Nebraska students sought to match faces and nationalities of 15 European countries, they were scored wrong in 93 percent of their identifications. (reference to a research report)

A. Complete the chart below with information from the article.

INFORMATION OR IDEA	TYPE OF SOURCE	NAME OR TITLE
failure of students in Nebraska (U.S.A.) to identify nationalities from photographs	research report	not given
stereotypes of childhood visions are very powerful	_____	not given
_____	writer and philosopher	William James
_____	_____	S.I. Hayakawa

B. Ask a partner the following questions. Imagine that your partner is an important professor, writer, or researcher. Take notes on his/her answers. Then write a sentence explaining your partner's BEST answer.

Example

A: Do you think that television is harmful to young children? Why or why not?

B: Yes, absolutely. Television keeps young children from learning to observe the world on their own.

According to (partner's name), a psychologist at (name of your school or university), television is definitely harmful to children because it keeps them from learning to observe the world on their own.

1. What is the most popular television show for children in your country?

2. Does the program stereotype one or more groups of people? How?

3. How can children and young people get rid of these stereotypes?

<u>According to</u>_____

_____

_____

Building Vocabulary

Using verbs as adjectives

Adjectives can be formed from many verbs by adding *-ing* or *-ed*. Note the difference in meaning:

I am very **confused** about the world.   (passive focus)

The world is very **confusing.**   (active focus)

A. Choose a word from the box to complete each sentence. Change the word into an adjective ending in -ing or -ed and write it in the sentence.

accustom	embarrass	impoverish
buzz	standardize	surprise

1. Stereotypes help give the world its <u>accustomed</u> look.

2. It is not _____ that stereotypes have something to do with prejudice.

3. Stereotypes are not only harmful but also _____ to the people who believe them.

4. It is not easy or quick for people to drop the _____ pictures in their minds.

5. The pictures we keep in our minds sometimes reveal some _____ facts.

6. William James said that the world is full of blooming, _____ confusion.

B. Give examples of each of the following.

1. something you find confusing: _____

2. something you are surprised about: _____

3. something you think is fascinating: _____

4. someone you are bored by: _____

5. two sports you consider exciting: _____

   and _____

Language Focus

Using relative clauses with <u>who</u>, <u>which</u>, or <u>that</u>
Relative clauses beginning with *who*, *which*, or *that* give more information about the nouns they follow. A relative clause must have its own subject and verb.

relative clause
The main thing *that distinguishes people with glasses* is just bad eyes.

Note: Not all clauses beginning with *that* are relative clauses. Noun clauses beginning with *that* are also used as sentence complements, for example:

noun clause
College students have revealed *that names conjure up the same images in their minds as they do in yours.*

A. Draw brackets [ ] around the relative clauses in the following sentences. Underline the noun that each relative clause describes.

1. The main thing [that distinguishes people with glasses] is just bad eyes.

2. Stereotypes are a kind of gossip about the world that makes us prejudge people before we see them.

3. The true process of change is a slow one which adds bits and pieces of reality to the pictures in our heads.

4. We are revealing the embarrassing facts which hang in the gallery of stereotypes in our heads.

B. Complete the relative clauses in these sentences with your own ideas.

1. Psychiatrists are doctors who _____

2. A stereotype is a generalization which _____

3. I dislike movies that _____

4. We should not trust judgments which _____

5. I admire people who _____

Discussion & Writing

1. Follow the process suggested by the author for getting rid of stereotypes.

   a. Think of a stereotype that many people in your culture believe. Explain how they grew up to believe this stereotype.

   b. Think of at least one exception to this stereotype.

   c. Explain how this stereotype might be harmful.

2. With a partner, conduct a survey of at least ten people you know. The object of the survey is to find out if the respondents can identify nationalities from pictures. Follow these steps:

   a. Cut out five photographs of people (not famous people) from an international magazine or newspaper. Be sure you know the nationality of the person in each photo.

   b. Ask each person to identify the nationality of the people in the pictures.

   c. Record the responses in the chart below.

PHOTO #1	PHOTO #2	PHOTO #3	PHOTO #4	PHOTO #5
Right: _____	_____	_____	_____	_____
Wrong: _____	_____	_____	_____	_____

   d. Write a brief summary of the results of your survey. What pictures did you choose? What percentage of the people you asked identified the photos correctly? What did you learn? Did anything surprise you?

Crossword Puzzle

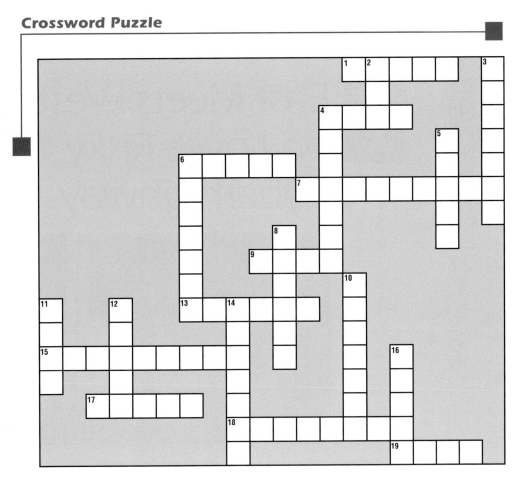

Use words from the reading to complete the crossword puzzle.

Across:

1 Having knowledge of
4 Person who feels superior to others
6 A kind of date
7 Prejudgment
9 Stereotype of French men
13 Informal talk about other people and their private lives
15 A kind of criminal
17 Light hair color
18 One who commits crimes
19 A lot: a good _____

Down:

2 Relative pronoun for people
3 Horn-rimmed _____
4 Having dark skin and hair
5 Relative pronoun for things
6 "The world is a blooming, _____ confusion."
8 To give meaning
10 Type of television show
11 Change in a negative way; distort
12 Uneducated country person
14 Start from _____
16 Place where we all live

Chapter 7

East Meets West on Love's Risky Cyberhighway

Yelena Khronina

How do I love thee?
Let me count the ways.
I love thee to the
*   depth and breadth*
*   and height*
My soul can reach,
When feeling out
*   of sight.*

—*Elizabeth Barrett Browning*
Poet
(1806–1861)

Chapter Focus

CONTENT:
Finding a husband or wife via the Internet

READING SKILL:
Recognizing diverse points of view

BUILDING VOCABULARY:
Using modifiers

LANGUAGE FOCUS
It's (not) + verb + -*ing*

Before You Read

1. The phrase "East Meets West" in the title of the article below refers to a famous line written by the English poet Rudyard Kipling (1865–1936):

   "Oh, East is East, and West is West, and never the twain shall meet."

   What do you think Kipling meant? Do you agree or disagree?

2. The "cyberhighway" in the title is the worldwide pathway of instant communication made possible by the Internet. How could such a highway have risks? What kind of risks do you think will be discussed in the article?

3. Some of the people described in the article say they are too busy for a social life because they work so many hours. Do you feel that you have enough time in your life for friendship and romantic relationships? Do most people in your country work too hard, too little, or just enough?

Reading Passage

EAST MEETS WEST ON LOVE'S RISKY CYBERHIGHWAY

by Fred Weir

from *The Christian Science Monitor*

1   Alevtina Ivanova and other Russian bachelorettes[1] like her are looking for **a few good men**—abroad. "Unfortunately, in our collapsed economy, very few men are able to support a family properly," she says. "Russian men lack confidence, they become
5   fatalistic,[2] they drink, they die young. It's not surprising that Russian women pin their hopes elsewhere."

---

[1] **bachelorette**   old-fashioned term for a young, unmarried woman

[2] **fatalistic**   accepting of the idea that everything is determined in advance; that individuals have no control over what happens in their lives

Ms. Ivanova, a veteran of half-a-dozen serious **cyber-relationships** with European and American men, is among thousands of Russian women turning to **the Internet** to meet
10 Westerners. The potential suitors[3] are equally frustrated with the dating prospects in their home countries.

"American women are too independent, too demanding, too critical," says Chris, a middle-aged US businessman visiting Moscow to meet "several very nice ladies" he contacted over **the Web**. The
15 visitor, who asked that his last name not be used, cites a joke often repeated here: "A Russian wife wants to keep house for you. An American wife wants to get rid of you, and keep the house."

Dozens of Web-based agencies are busy playing **match-maker**, for fees paid by both the women, who send in their pictures and bios[4] for
20 posting on international Websites, and the men, who can obtain contact information for the women who pique their interest.[5]

Though there are no firm statistics, it is estimated that between 4,000 and 6,000 women from the **former USSR** marry US citizens each year. One agency currently lists 25,000 women from Russia and
25 other former Soviet republics seeking Western mates; there are dozens more agencies, each offering thousands of would-be brides.[6] Some agencies have branched into travel, translation and other services to profit from what they say is an exploding traffic.

While some describe these international e-introductions as
30 offering matches made in heaven,[7] others see nightmares in cyberspace. "People bring their illusions as well as their dreams to this market,"[8] says Tatiana Gurko, head of the independent Center for Gender Studies in Moscow. "Like any physical place, the Internet has predators[9] lurking about, and sometimes they may be hard to spot."

35 Western men increasingly report being ripped off[10] by wily Russian women, who write sweet e-mails, send sexy digital photos, hit them up for cash,[11] and then disappear.

---

[3] **potential suitors**   men they may possibly meet who would like to form romantic relationships

[4] **bio**   short form of biography, a summary of one's life

[5] **pique their interest**   attract them

[6] **would-be brides**   women who would like to get married

[7] **matches made in heaven**   ideal, perfect relationships

[8] **this market**   this place for them to contact each other

[9] **predators**   here, people who hurt others

[10] **ripped off**   cheated; swindled

[11] **hit (someone) up for cash**   ask someone for money

On the other side, tales filtering back to Russia of Internet marriages gone sour[12]—including the murder of a Russian **e-mail-order** bride in the US—have put women on their guard.

But Ivanova, who now works as an adviser to DiOritz, a large Moscow matchmaking agency, says that, although none of her cyber-relationships have led to marriage, she has had no regrettable experiences.

"You can find out everything you need to know about a man in five e-mails," she says breezily. "Men are fairly obvious, you just need to question them properly." To her, the requirements on both sides are clear: "A woman need only be attractive and educated, but a man must have property, means, and a good job."

Yelena Khronina, who plans to soon wed "a wonderful Norwegian man" she met via the Internet, says her dream has come true. "It's so hard to be a woman in Russia," Ms. Khronina sighs. "But then you visit this beautiful, orderly, prosperous country, and spend time with a man who treats you with kindness and respect. Why would anyone say no to that?"

The potential dangers of dabbling in cyberromance[13] are dramatized in a recent film, *Birthday Girl*, in which Nicole Kidman plays a mail-order bride from Moscow who brings a gang of Russian **mafia** thugs[14] crashing into the life of her English bank-clerk beau. In real life, the sting is usually more mundane:[15] An unsuspecting Western man falls in love after a few gushing[16] e-mail exchanges with a false identity[17] posted on a Website—sometimes the photos are actually of a Russian actress or fashion model—and is persuaded to wire cash for a ticket to visit him, or to meet some personal emergency.

"A woman can string a man along,[18] playing on his emotions and sympathy and, in doing so, trick him into giving her money or expensive items," says Paul O'Brien, a US Web designer who has temporarily given up his search for a Russian wife after being burned[19] by two women who just wanted money from him.

---

[12] **gone sour**   ruined; ended in separation or divorce

[13] **dabbling in cyberromance**   experimenting with romance online; trying it out

[14] **thugs**   violent criminals

[15] **mundane**   ordinary

[16] **gushing**   overly sweet and wordy

[17] **false identity**   fake person, someone who does not exist

[18] **string a man along**   fool him into believing she loves him

[19] **burned**   disappointed in love; heartbroken

70   Mr. O'Brien says he resorted to the Internet because of America's fast-paced, impersonal and workaholic[20] culture. "A lot of guys I know work many, many hours and do not have time for a social life," he says. "So it seems particularly appealing to them when these agencies offer to help them make contact with beautiful and single

75   women," he says, but warns: "Prospective suitors need to be very wary of the women out there who have no intention of developing a relationship with them."

Russian women insist it is they who face the greatest hazards. Many have heard about Anastasia Solovyova, a Russian from the

80   former Soviet republic of Kyrgyztan, who was murdered by her American husband two years ago. She had been his second mail-order bride. Experts say there are many more tales of miserable, and sometimes tragic, mismatches.

"You come to a strange country, to meet a man you've only

85   corresponded with by e-mail," says Ivanova. "There are issues of language, culture, and personal morality. It takes a lot of trust, and for some women it goes badly wrong."

The terrorist attacks of **September 11**, which brought the Russian and US governments closer together may, paradoxically,[21] have put at

90   least a temporary damper on the love fest.[22]

Tamara Babkina, deputy director of Wedding Palace No. 4, which is the only office in Moscow where foreigners can legally marry, says that until last year, Americans were the largest group marrying Russian women. "We had 175 US–Russian weddings in 2001, but since

95   September 11 there has not been a single one," Ms. Babkina says.

While no one wants to go on the record[23] criticizing love, some experts argue that the Westward outflow of Russian women must be viewed as a baneful social indicator.[24]

"Russia has become the world's leading exporter of wives, and this

100   is a tremendously profitable business," says Ms. Gurko.

---

[20] **workaholic**   addicted to work

[21] **paradoxically**   contrary to what you expect

[22] **put a damper on the love fest**   make the atmosphere (here, dating) less cheerful or pleasant

[23] **go on the record**   say publicly

[24] **baneful social indicator**   troubling sign that something is wrong in a society

"It may be a real **supply-and-demand** situation," she says, "but let's try to remember that this vast supply of terrific women is made up of individuals whose hopes have been crushed in Russia.

"It's so sad that, in order to seek a better life, a Russian woman has
105 to leave."

About the Source

The *Christian Science Monitor* is an international daily newspaper published Monday through Friday in Boston, Massachusetts. Founded in 1908, the *CS Monitor* features international news stories, but also contains U.S. news and human interest stories.

After You Read

Understanding the Text

A. Main idea. Read the three paragraphs below, then choose the one which best summarizes the main ideas of the article. Circle the number next to your choice.

1. With the help of Web-based agencies, thousands of Russian women are seeking husbands abroad, primarily in the United States and Western Europe. While many of the relationships are reported to have happy endings, there are also risks involved on both sides. The fact that so many Russian women want to leave their country to get married is one indicator of the country's serious economic and social problems.

2. Alevtina Ivanova is a young Russian woman who has tried unsuccessfully to find a European or American husband with property, means, and a good job. She doesn't want to marry a Russian man, so she expects to keep looking until she finds the ideal husband. Ivanova is aware of the dangers, but feels that the rewards far outweigh the risks.

3. The dangers of trying to find a romantic partner via the Internet are great for both Russian women and American men. There are many issues that can go badly wrong. The case of the Russian woman who was murdered by her American husband is well known, and there are many more cyber-relationships that end in divorce. It is also common for Russian women to rip off American men.

B. Supporting ideas. Put a check (√) next to the supporting ideas, details, and examples included in the article.

1. __√__   It is estimated that between 4,000 and 6,000 women from the former U.S.S.R. marry U.S. citizens each year.

2. _____   American women are increasingly fed up with American men and are looking for husbands in Western Europe.

3. _____   Internet dating services are very popular in Asia.

4. _____   Some Western men have been cheated out of money by Russian women who post beautiful photographs but have false identities.

5. _____   In 2001, Norwegians were the second largest group marrying Russian women.

6. _____   One Russian e-mail-order bride was murdered by her American husband.

7. _____   Some of the matchmaking agencies now operating in Russia are not licensed by the government and cannot be trusted.

8. _____   Russia has become the world's leading exporter of wives.

C. Consider the issues. Work with a partner to answer the questions below.

1. Alevtina Ivanova is critical of Russian men's ability to support a family. Specifically, what does she NOT like about them? Tell your partner.

2. Based on your answer to question 1, what can you infer that Alevtina likes about Westerners? Do you agree that these are important qualities for a prospective husband? Discuss them with your partner.

3. What about men in your country? Do you think Alevtina would approve of them as potential husbands? Why or why not?

> **Recognizing diverse points of view**
>
> The author of a piece of writing always has a **point of view,** a position from which he or she sees what is going on in the story. In newspaper and magazine articles, the author's point of view is usually neutral. That is, the writer does not openly express an opinion on the issues or events described in the article, but tries to summarize the points of view of other people. In this way, readers will be able to see what is going on from several angles and then draw their own conclusions.

A. Look back at the reading and identify the person expressing each of the following points of view. Where possible, add a phrase that gives more information about the person.

1. People who use dating services sometimes fool themselves into thinking that their dreams will come true.

Tatiana Gurko, head of the independent Center for Gender

Studies

2. My dream has come true. I am very happy to be leaving Russia to marry a Norwegian man.

_____

_____

3. I give up. I've tried to develop a relationship with a beautiful single woman over the Internet but have been burned twice.

_____

_____

4. American women are not my type. I'd prefer a Russian wife.

_____

_____

5. Although I have not met the husband of my dreams, I have no regrets.

_____

_____

Using modifiers

Modifiers are descriptive words (adjectives) that often come before nouns. Modifiers answer questions like, *How many...?*, *How large...?*, *What kind...?*, *Where from...?*, and *How good...?*

> *Western* men increasingly report being ripped off by *wily Russian* women, who write *sweet* e-mails, send *sexy digital* photos, hit them up for cash, and then disappear.

Modifiers may also come after the nouns they describe. Verbs such as *be, seem, appear, become,* or *feel* (linking verbs) are used to link modifiers to the nouns they describe.

> A woman need only be *attractive* and *educated*...

Other modifiers are made from verbs (*exploding* traffic, *collapsed* economy) or from combinations of words connected by a hyphen (*mail-order* bride, *Moscow-based* agency).

A. In the following sentences, underline the words that modify nouns.

1. American women are too independent, too demanding, too critical.

2. The potential suitors are equally frustrated with the dating prospects in their home countries.

3. A woman need only be attractive and educated, but a man must have property, means, and a good job.

4. But then you visit this beautiful, orderly, prosperous country, and spend time with a man who treats you with kindness and respect.

5. In real life, the sting is usually more mundane.

6. Let's try to remember that this vast supply of terrific women is made up of individuals whose hopes have been crushed in Russia.

> ### It's (not) + verb + -ing
> In sentences beginning with *It's...* or *It's not...*, we can use the
> active participle form (verb + *-ing*) of some verbs to describe how
> we think people feel about something.
>
> > *It's not surprising* that Russian women pin their hopes
> > elsewhere.
> > (It doesn't surprise most people..., Most people are not
> > surprised...)
>
> The same type of sentence may also be introduced with *The fact
> that...* or *The idea that...*
>
> > *The fact that* Russian women pin their hopes elsewhere *is not
> > surprising.*

A. Complete the following sentences with opinions of your own.

   1. It's interesting that _____

   2. It's disgusting that _____

   3. It's amazing that _____

   4. It must be upsetting to be _____

B. Use verb + *-ing* to express your opinion about the following facts.

   1. It's not _____ that some Russian women do
     not like American men.

   2. The fact that people are so busy that they don't have time for
     dating is _____.

   3. The idea of finding a husband or wife via the Internet is
     _____.

1. Reread the last three paragraphs of the article (pages 78–79). Do you think a business that exports wives from a country should be allowed by international law? Why or why not?

2. In the reading, Alevtina Ivanova says you can find out everything you need to know about a man in five e-mails (lines 45–46). In order for her plan to work, the **purpose** of each e-mail to a prospective suitor must be crystal clear to the writer. For example:

E-mail number	Purpose
1.	find out if he has a good job
2.	find out if he owns a house
3.	find out if he is good-looking

Work with a partner. What things do you think it is important to know about a potential husband or wife? Decide on the five most important requirements. Write them in the chart below.

HUSBANDS	WIVES
_____	_____
_____	_____
_____	_____
_____	_____

3. Imagine that you are writing a letter or e-mail to a prospective mate in another country. Choose one of the requirements in your chart above and, keeping your purpose in mind, try to find out if the person has what you are looking for. (Hint: keep in mind the cultural differences that might apply. For example, it is impolite in some cultures to ask direct questions about salary and property.)

Crossword Puzzle

Use words from the reading to complete the crossword puzzle.

Across:

3 Someone seeking a romantic relationship

4 Actress Nicole _____

5 Capital of Russia

8 Very, very sad

9 Boyfriend, sweetheart

10 Opposite of sweet

12 Criminal organization

13 Supply and _____

14 "An American wife wants to get _____ of you and keep the house."

15 To send outside of a country

17 The World Wide _____

18 Person from another country

Down:

1 Old-fashioned term for a young, unmarried woman

2 A person who is addicted to work

6 Wealthy and successful

7 Ordinary, everyday things

11 Some customers are worried about getting ripped _____.

12 _____-order bride

16 Never the _____ shall meet

Chapter **8**

Students Won't Give Up Their French Fries

*He who distinguishes
the true savor of
his food can never
be a glutton;
he who does not
cannot be otherwise.*

—Henry David Thoreau
Philosopher and naturalist
(1817–1862)

Chapter Focus

CONTENT:
American students' obsession with food

READING SKILL:
Scanning for specific information

BUILDING VOCABULARY:
Idiomatic expressions

LANGUAGE FOCUS:
Reported speech

86 *Chapter 8* • *Students Won't Give Up Their French Fries*

Before You Read

1. Do you have a healthy diet? Why or why not?

2. Read the title of the article and then take one minute to skim the text. What do you think the article will be about? Share your ideas with a partner.

3. Where do most students in your college or university eat? What does a typical meal consist of? What do students eat between meals? Are they generally concerned about health and nutrition while they are in college? Why or why not?

Reading Passage

STUDENTS WON'T GIVE UP
THEIR FRENCH FRIES

by Elizabeth F. Farrell

from *The Chronicle of Higher Education*

1   On a recent summer night at the local **Dairy Queen** in Moorhead, Minnesota, Debra Lee-Cadwell, the director of dining services at **Concordia College,** felt a tap on her shoulder. She turned around to find a young man she didn't recognize holding up an ice-cream cone.

5   "He asked me if it was a red, yellow, or green," says **Ms. Lee-Cadwell**, who realized the young man was a student at Concordia, where she has added color-coded labels to all dining-hall foods to inform students of fat content. Yellow means low fat (less than 5 grams), green indicates medium fat content (5 to 13 grams), and red
10   is for high-fat foods (more than 13 grams).

"I told him it was a red, but that was OK, as long as it was in moderation," says Ms. Lee-Cadwell, who is a **registered dietitian**.

Perhaps it is an attempt to avoid gaining the dreaded "freshman 15,"[1] but students around the country are demanding more
15 information about the foods they're served in dining halls, and they're asking for a greater variety of healthy fare, according to college officials. Over the past few years, colleges have responded by hiring more dietitians and nutritionists and going to greater lengths[2] to provide students with information about the caloric and fat content
20 of the food they eat.

But despite the wealth of information, students don't appear to be eating any healthier than their predecessors.[3]

"They may be more health conscious, but that doesn't necessarily mean that they're eating healthy," says Robin L. Porter, the president
25 of H. David Porter Associates Inc., an independent food consulting business based in Crofton, Maryland, that works with 70 colleges. "They talk the talk, but don't really walk the walk[4]—french fries outsell apples by thousands and thousands of pounds."

Some even worry that the feast of information can be harmful, by
30 feeding some students' obsession[5] with food.

Information and Options
Several colleges have recently purchased software called NetNutrition, from the Ithaca-based company CBord, which allows students to click through the dining-hall menus on their college's Web
35 site and learn the preparation method, ingredients, nutrients, and health information for every dish served.

For example, a student at the **University of Southern California** using the Web site one day this month could have chosen among Thai beef salad (144 calories,[6] 4.2 grams of fat), vegetarian sloppy joes[7]
40 (362 calories, 5.1 grams of fat), and Japanese spinach (at 47 calories, 1.9 grams of fat), or opted for classic American favorites like cheeseburgers (436 calories, 35.8 grams of fat) and pepperoni pizza (241 calories, 18 grams of fat), to name a few dishes. USC has even

---

[1] **the dreaded freshman 15** 15 pounds (6.8 kilograms) that American students fear they will gain during their first year at college or university

[2] **going to greater lengths** trying much harder

[3] **predecessors** those who were students before them

[4] **they talk the talk, but don't really walk the walk** (slang) they don't do what they say they are going to do

[5] **obsession** something they cannot stop thinking about

[6] **calories** units for measuring the energy that a certain amount of food will provide

[7] **sloppy joes** sandwich made of ground beef mixed with tomato sauce; vegetarian style is made with soy

set up kiosks[8] in one of its dining halls to allow students to check the
45 Web site with their dinner trays in hand, and other colleges are
installing similar kiosks.

Even at USC, however, pizza is still the most popular item, says
Michael P. Gratz, the director of hospitality services. He says burgers
and fries are being consumed as much as ever.

50 **More Variety**
It's not that students lack food options. The university's 29 dining
halls boast condiment[9] bars with **kimchi** and four different types of
mayonnaise.

"Ethnic[10] foods and ingredients are also increasingly popular," says
55 Haddon Reines, vice president of health care and education for U.S.
FoodService Inc., a food distributor based in Columbia, Maryland.
"Students have grown up eating a wider array of foods, and it's no
longer uncommon for sushi to be in dining halls."

Fries and a Coke
60 Still, the three items that top U.S. FoodService's list of most
frequently ordered foods are chicken tenders,[11] french fries, and
carbonated beverages.[12]

"Some days I feel like I'm banging my head against a wall,"[13] says Ms.
Lee-Cadwell of Concordia, which is also setting up electronic kiosks.
65 "The students talk out of both sides of their mouths. They say they
want nutrition and variety, but then they gravitate to their familiar
favorites—the pizza, the burgers, and the fried chicken strips."

Or they take an opposite approach, nutrition experts say, and
become so preoccupied with food that they barely eat anything.

70 "There definitely seems to be two extremes," says Stephanie
Horvath, a senior at the **University of North Carolina** at Chapel
Hill. "A lot of people eat the burgers and fries … and then there are
people who grasp onto what they think is healthy and don't eat
balanced meals."

---

[8] **kiosk**   a small counter or booth with computers where students can get information

[9] **condiment**   an extra substance like sauce or seasoning added to food to improve its flavor

[10] **ethnic**   of a particular racial or cultural group

[11] **chicken tenders**   breaded and fried strips of chicken meat

[12] **carbonated beverages**   flavored drinks with chemically produced bubbles (such as Coca-Cola, Pepsi, etc.)

[13] **banging my head against a wall**   trying without success

75   Ms. Horvath recalls that her two roommates freshman year would brag about how "good" they had been on a given day because they ate nothing but a piece of bread. Another friend ate only salads, and "couldn't figure out why she always had stomach aches and digestive problems," says Ms. Horvath.

80   What Ms. Horvath and many college dietitians and nutritionists observe is part of a national trend. Although it is difficult to say what percentage of college students have eating disorders[14] or struggle with obesity,[15] many college nutritionists say they notice a growing number of students splitting into two camps of unhealthy eaters:
85   overweight fast-food junkies, or obsessive dieters, who either binge and purge[16] or nearly starve themselves.

      "It's sort of like everything else in our country," says Christine D. Economos, an assistant professor of nutrition at **Tufts University** who specializes in the study of college students' eating habits.
90   "There's a public health crisis with obesity, and there's also more eating disorders, and in both cases the underlying cause is the same in that it's emotional and started before they set foot on campus."

Striving for Moderation

      The problems of compulsive overeating and undereating[17] have the
95   same underlying cause, health officials say: They both show an inability to eat in moderation. Consequently, experts like Ronda Bokram, the staff nutritionist at the student health center at **Michigan State University**, say the availability of nutritional information does little or nothing to influence students' eating habits.

100   The students who should be paying attention to nutritional information are ignoring it, Ms. Bokram says, while the ones that pay attention care too much.

      "I would do anything to get rid of things like kiosks," says Ms. Bokram. "I have students say they won't eat foods that have a certain
105   amount of fat grams in them, and that's just unhealthy. I think giving students that information sends the wrong message. … It's important to teach people to eat without labels."

      Students tend to disagree. Lindsey McAdams, a senior at **Meredith College**, in Raleigh, N.C., says that she wishes the dining halls at her
110   college provided such information. If it had been available, she adds, it

---

[14] **eating disorders**   serious medical conditions related to food and body image

[15] **obesity**   condition of being overweight

[16] **binge and purge**   overeat and then make themselves vomit

[17] **compulsive overeating and undereating**   unable to resist eating too much or eating too little all the time

might have helped her make more informed eating decisions her freshman year, when she gained more than 30 pounds.

And Ms. Horvath, at Chapel Hill, points out that such information is no different from labels on foods in the supermarket.

115 "If they're going to make it mandatory[18] for you to be on meal plan, they have an obligation to tell you what's in the food they're serving," she says.

Meanwhile, college nutritionists and dietitians will continue to emphasize moderation as a key to healthy eating, both at college and 120 beyond.

As Nancy Ellson, a nutritionist at **William Paterson University**, in Wayne, N.J., puts it: "It's easy to give the students nutritional information, but it's hard to impart to them the understanding that food is the one thing they have to make peace with in their lives. ... 125 Unlike other things they may develop addictions to, food is the one thing they can't give up for the rest of their lives."

About the Source

The *Chronicle of Higher Education* is a weekly newspaper that features news about American colleges and universities. With a circulation of approximately 450,000, The *Chronicle* also reports on the latest developments in research, information technology, and on government policies that affect colleges and their students.

After You Read

Understanding the Text

A. Multiple choice. For each item below, circle the **two** best answers.

1. American students are demanding more information about the food they eat at college because _____.

   a. they are concerned about nutrition

   b. they want to eat more international foods

   c. they don't want to gain weight

   d. their parents want to pay less

---

[18] **mandatory**   required

2. Colleges have responded to students' concerns by _____.
   a. providing students with more information about caloric and fat content of foods
   b. making more burgers and fries available after hours
   c. providing diet and exercise programs to help students lose weight
   d. hiring more dietitians and nutritionists

3. The fact that french fries outsell apples by thousands of pounds implies that despite students' apparent interest in eating healthy foods, _____.
   a. they are eating more fruits and vegetables
   b. they are beginning to enjoy more ethnic foods
   c. they are not eating more healthy foods
   d. they are not cutting down on fatty foods

4. The ways colleges and universities provide nutrition information to students include _____.
   a. adding color-coded labels to dining-hall foods
   b. setting computer kiosks where students can check nutrition Websites
   c. adding a wide variety of international and ethnic foods
   d. playing videos in the dining halls that promote healthy living

5. Recent studies of eating habits of American college students indicate that many young people have problems with _____.
   a. their roommates
   b. obesity
   c. eating disorders
   d. money

6. Public health experts agree that eating disorders _____.
   a. are caused by poor nutrition
   b. are caused by emotional problems
   c. are a major issue on American campuses
   d. begin when students arrive on campus

B. Consider the issues. Work with a partner to answer the questions below.

1. According to the article, some experts are worried that making too much information about nutrition available to students can actually be harmful. Do you agree or disagree? Why?

2. Considering the wide variety of food options available at colleges and universities in the United States (lines 37–58), do you think students there have the opportunity to eat well? Why or why not?

3. In lines 94–96, the author states that the problems related to overeating and undereating are both caused by the inability to eat in moderation. Why do you think that so many American students have this problem?

Reading Skill

Scanning for specific information
When you need to find specific information in a text, you should scan it, or move your eyes very quickly across the text without reading every word, stopping only to "pick up" the information you are looking for.

A. Scan the text on pages 87–91 to find the specific information below. Remember to look quickly over the text without reading every word.

1. Who is the director of dining services at Concordia College?

   _____

2. How many grams of fat are in a high-fat food?

   _____

3. What is the name of the software that allows students to click through dining-hall menus on their college's Website?

   _____

4. How many calories are in a serving of Thai beef salad?

   _____

5. What is the most popular food item at USC (University of Southern California)?

   _____

B. The Web page below is maintained by the **Centers for Disease Control and Prevention** (CDC), an agency of the U.S. government that seeks to improve public health. *Scan it to find these things:*

1. What two types of foods does the CDC hope that more people will consume more of? _____ and _____

2. How many servings per day of these foods does the CDC recommend? _____

3. By what year does the program expect to achieve its goal?

   _____

4. Which organizations have sponsored research related to the program? _____ and _____

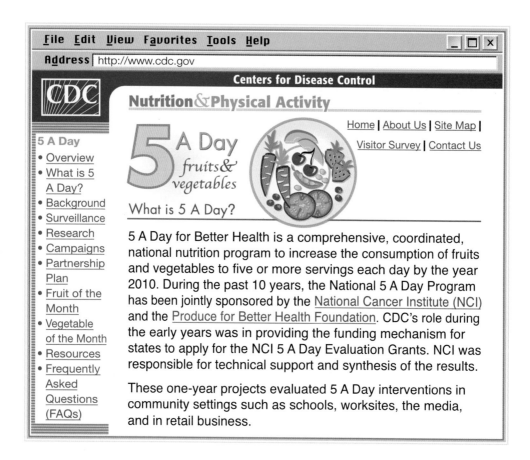

Idiomatic expressions

Newspaper and magazine articles often include idiomatic expressions that people use in ordinary conversation. Many of these are direct quotations from people the author has interviewed. When you see a new expression, pay careful attention to the sentence you find it in. You may also find clues to the meaning of the expression in the sentences that come before or after it. Paying close attention to the context that surrounds a new expression can help you figure out its meaning and remember it.

The sentences below contain idiomatic expressions (in **boldface** type). Read the whole sentence and choose the best meaning for the expression. Circle the letter for your answer.

1. "The students **talk out of both sides of their mouths.** They say they want nutrition and variety, but then they gravitate to their familiar favorites."

   a. talk while they are eating

   b. support each other

   c. say one thing but do another

2. "A lot of people eat the burgers and fries … and then there are people who **grasp onto** what they think is healthy and don't eat balanced meals."

   a. give up

   b. strongly believe in

   c. don't care

3. "There's a public-health crisis with obesity, and there's also more eating disorders, and in both cases the underlying cause is the same in that it's emotional and started before they **set foot on campus.**"

   a. apply to a university or college

   b. arrive at university or college

   c. join an exercise program at the college

Reported speech

Writers use **reported speech** to report what someone else said without repeating their exact words:

> Students say, "We won't give up our french fries." (direct quotation)

> Students say that they won't give up their french fries. (reported speech)

In reported speech, we usually use a clause beginning with *that*, or, if the reported speech is in the form of a question, a clause beginning with *what, where, when, if,* or *whether.*

> "What do you eat for breakfast?" she asked.

> She asked me what I eat for breakfast.

Tense sequence in reported statements and questions (when the verb in the direct quotation is present):

Main Verb	Reported Speech Verb
present *(students say)* ⟶	no change *(they won't)*
past *(she asked me)* ⟶	past *(I ate)* or present *(I eat)**

*especially when the verb expresses repeated or habitual action

A. Underline the reported speech clauses in the following sentences.

1. He asked me if it was red, yellow, or green.

2. The director of hospitality services says that pizza is still the most popular item.

3. At one university, students complained that only unhealthy options were available.

4. In a survey of students' food habits, nutritionists asked students whether they ate fast foods or healthy foods more frequently.

5. A senior at the University of North Carolina reported that on some days many of her friends ate only bread.

B. Ask a partner three questions about his or her eating habits. Use present tense verbs to ask the questions. Record both the questions you asked and your partner's answers in the chart below.

QUESTIONS	ANSWERS
Direct: "What do you eat for breakfast?" **Reported:** <u>I asked her what she eats for breakfast.</u>	**Direct:** She said, "I usually eat a bowl of cereal." **Reported:** She said that she usually eats a bowl of cereal.

Discussion & Writing

1. Based on what you have read in the article, would you want to live at a college or university in the United States? Why or why not?

2. **Group work.** Work with a small group of your classmates to do one of the following:

   a. Compare the nutritional information on the two labels below. Report your findings to the class.

Vanilla Ice Cream		*Nori-Maki*	
Nutrition Facts Serving Size 4 oz. (450 g)		**Nutrition Facts** Serving Size 6 pieces (100 g)	
Amount Per Serving		Amount Per Serving	
Calories	100	Calories	97
Fat	3 g	Fat	3 g
Cholesterol	35 mg	Cholesterol	20 mg
Sodium	10 mg	Sodium	72 mg
Carbohydrate	16 g	Carbohydrate	12 g
Protein	2 g	Protein	6 g

   b. Look through a popular magazine for teenagers or young adults. What types of food are advertised? Choose one ad and describe it to the class.

3. Imagine that you have a friend who is about to leave to study at one of the colleges or universities mentioned in the article. Write a letter to your friend explaining what you learned about the eating habits of American students and offering some friendly advice.

Crossword Puzzle

Use words from the reading to complete the crossword puzzle.

Across:

1 Chutney and ketchup, for example
4 Something to drink
6 Between two _____
7 Don't bang your _____ against a wall
10 Popular junk food on U.S. campuses
11 A unit of energy
13 Very popular Japanese dish
14 A place to get information
16 Eat more than is good for you

Down:

2 The way something looks
3 Student in the first year of college
5 Belonging to a particular cultural group
8 Students living in the same room
9 Pickled Korean cabbage
12 Something you can't stop thinking about
15 Foods like ice cream and french fries are high in this

Chapter ▲ **9**

Getting Into the Game

*You can be in
my world if I can
be in yours.*

—Bob Dylan
*Songwriter and performer
(1942–   )*

Before You Read

1. Read the description of English author **Lewis Carroll's** stories about a little girl named Alice. Discuss the questions below.

Lewis Carroll first thought of the character known around the world as Alice in Wonderland to amuse a little girl. The two books that grew out of his original stories, *Alice's Adventures in Wonderland* and its continuation, *Through the Looking Glass*, have also given immense pleasure to adults and have been translated into more than 30 languages. In Carroll's fantasy, Alice follows a rabbit (the White Rabbit) down a hole and finds herself in a make-believe world filled with strange characters, including the Cheshire Cat, the Mad Hatter, the Duchess, and the Queen of Hearts. The language of the stories often seems like nonsense, containing many figures of speech and funny plays on words. Some of these are so well known that people use them in everyday conversation. Today, the story of Alice remains one of the most popular in English literature.

> Have you heard of the character, Alice in Wonderland? How much of the story do you remember? Which characters were your favorites?

2. Scan through the article on pages 101–105 for quotations from Lewis Carroll's stories. Why do you think the author chose to include these quotations in her article?

3. Do you enjoy playing electronic games? Which ones? What do you like or dislike about electronic games in general?

GETTING INTO THE GAME

by Gloria Goodale

from *The Christian Science Monitor*

Alice was so astonished that she couldn't speak
for a minute: it quite seemed to take her breath away.
—*Through the Looking Glass* by Lewis Carroll

1   This story is for every adult who's never had reason to play video
games and thinks that's all they are—just games. You need to come
with me, as Alice did with the White Rabbit, into a world you've never
imagined. Since diving into the rabbit hole of gaming[1] a few years
5   ago, I've come to believe this is not just some trivial, peripheral
world. It's the world that is coming, a world that is taking over the
one in which you and I grew up. And a wonderland it is, plus some.

I began writing about video games sort of the way Alice stumbled
upon Carroll's rabbit hole. I was simply following the inescapable,
10   supremely compelling "white rabbits" in my life, namely my kids. I
wanted to know why these two would disappear to stare at these
games for as long as I'd allow.

Ever since I started fumbling with joysticks and game controllers, I
feel I've been falling slow-motion into a place I didn't really
15   understand or appreciate. Like some kind of late-bloomer,[2] I've also
been having a slow-motion "Aha!"[3]

This, I'm discovering, is a world in which choice is the rule,
boundaries shift at will, and experimentation is the norm. It is a world
in which the player defines the "story," not an omnipotent author.[4] And
20   it's changing the way our children are growing up, the way they see
themselves, and, ultimately, after years of interactive entertainment,
the way they think and the society they're going to create.

If these seem like big thoughts for a gaming industry that
the mainstream press[5] largely dismisses as harmful, violent,

---

[1] **diving into the rabbit hole of gaming**   entering the imaginary world
of playing video games

[2] **late-bloomer**   a person who discovers or does interesting things late in
life

[3] **Aha!**   an exclamation meaning, "Oh, now I understand!"

[4] **an omnipotent author**   an author who has complete control of the story

[5] **the mainstream press**   newspapers, magazines, and television news
channels that represent the dominant trend in trends and opinion

25 testosterone-loaded[6] escapism, consider this. Video games are expected to be a $31 billion industry by the end of this year, several times as big as the world's film industry. And violent games make up less than 10 percent of all those played.

But I digress.[7] What I really want is to get you to float with me
30 awhile past these new cultural signposts[8] to see if you come to the same conclusions.

Since talking creatures are very much a part of that world, I thought we'd use some of Carroll's characters as guides along the way.

"Tell me which way I ought to walk from here?" asked Alice.

35 *"That," the Cheshire Cat replied, "depends a good deal on where you want to get to."*

The first stop is "Seaman," by **Sega**. This console game uses voice-recognition technology to enable a cyber-creature to "hear" and respond to the players. The goal is to create and raise a creature that
40 is half man, half fish. My (nearly) teenage son and I take on the challenge together.

We hatch a pea-sized egg that we have to lay in a watery womb with a delicate enough touch to allow it to stick to the sides and begin growing. A thermometer and light meter beep at us hourly when the
45 zygote[9] has gotten too cold or has too much light. Even so, we kill at least a dozen before we finally manage to get the darn thing to adhere and begin growing.

But given the fact that my son and I have other things to do in a day, like school and work, we flop numerous times during this stage,
50 as well. By the time we produce a surly, adult cyber-pet, we feel as if we have created a new life, written a new story in which we are characters.

We try to encourage our cyber-pet to think about poetry or what he wants to do when he, it, grows up. It proves to be as strong-willed and
55 demanding as any flesh-and-blood charge I've ever cared for. And it yells at us in English, not woofs and meows.[10]

"Feed me!" "I'm REALLY COLD!!!!"

---

[6] **testosterone-loaded** filled with elements that have special appeal to boys and men

[7] **But I digress.** But I am getting off the main subject.

[8] **these new cultural signposts** these new indications that society may be changing

[9] **zygote** a fertilized, growing egg

[10] **woofs and meows** the sounds made by real dogs and cats

After several days of anguish,[11] we decide to let it die. Homework lies unfinished. We must move on. We are relieved but guilt-ridden. My son shakes his head and says, "I never realized a pet required so much attention."

I have just achieved the golden ring of parenting.[12] My offspring has learned to care for someone other than himself, and I have not had to flush a single, real goldfish down the toilet in the service of that lesson.

"Get to your places!" shouted the Queen in a voice of thunder, and people began running about in all directions.

Next stop is "**The Sims**," dubbed a "God-game" because participants, playing on their computers, can create and control the cyber-universes of small towns, discotheques, birthday parties, or whatever else appeals to them. I watch and learn as my teenage daughter creates an **extended family** that argues all the time ("You need a haircut!" "I need more money!" "You don't love me anymore!"). She makes them have children, burn down their house, go bankrupt,[13] kill a person, go to jail, and come back to life. She soon learns that even cyber-life isn't as easy to control as she'd like, however.

So she starts the process over, hoping to direct her family into new, more productive channels. "I had no idea how hard it was to be a grown-up," she says to me.

This is a game in which the player has to make lots of decisions, each taking the story in a new direction. In that sense, it's also a game that departs from the linear concept of storytelling[14] in place for several thousand years of Western literature. By writing her own story the player becomes author. It's a far cry from the world of childhood tales with the same ending (and moral lesson) each time.

Think about the implications of that for a while.

"Be what you would seem to be," says the Duchess.

The online world is our last stop. I decide to brave the recently launched game, "Magic: The Gathering Online," by myself, although my son joins me shortly.

In "Magic," players are mythical figures or avatars[15] who battle to the death with enchanted creatures and other magical folks, using

---

[11] **anguish**   great mental suffering; distress

[12] **the golden ring of parenting**   the highest goal a parent can achieve

[13] **go bankrupt**   become unable to pay one's debts

[14] **linear concept of storytelling**   way of telling stories in which events happen in order, as if arranged in a line

[15] **mythical figures or avatars**   characters with special, superhuman powers

spells[16] and unpredictable powers. My avatar appears at a wooden table onscreen and waits.

95   This is the cyber-equivalent of standing in your front yard and yelling into your neighborhood, "Does anybody want to play with me?"

Miraculously, someone does, despite the fact that I don't have a name like "Screamin' Wolf" or "Panther." I have not mastered the spells, I don't know how to block the plagues and ogres[17] he throws
100   at me, and I die fast. I quickly get a new name, "Alice," and whip up[18] a new avatar, a sort of startled-looking **Amelia Earhart** figure. That's an improvement, I think.

It is only when my son joins the game that I begin to fully appreciate yet another dimension of the online, interactive bonding.
105   First, he has to overcome the "handicap"[19] of playing under his mother's online "face." Your cyber-identity is very important, I understand, but since I will not pay for two online accounts, he has to learn a tad[20] of humility.

Alice, he is. But the first thing he does is send an onscreen instant
110   message, part of the game, to tell his new cyberspace opponent, ViperBat, that he is playing under his mother's name. They proceed to throw spells and wild creatures at each other, each strategizing, each winning and losing at equal rates.

In between hexes,[21] a conversation begins to flow between my son
115   and what turns out to be a 16-year-old boy in Ohio. They trade game tips and console each other over how badly each plays. Once the game ends, they can locate each other and play again anytime.

Herein lies another "Aha!" moment for me.

Multiply such friendships by the current 20-million online players
120   worldwide, says futurist Don Tapscott, and you have the seed of a new kind of community.

And it all starts between one person here and one anywhere. Says Jenkins, "I have students who play with Koreans hourly, not daily. The potential to transform international relationships can be very
125   significant because games can be done visually, not necessarily in language.

---

[16] **spells**   words with magical powers

[17] **block the plagues and ogres**   defend myself from illnesses and evil monsters

[18] **whip up**   quickly create

[19] **"handicap"**   what he thinks of as a disadvantage

[20] **a tad**   a little

[21] **hexes**   curses; evil spells

He invokes the early 20th-century dream of a universal language: "Games are the new **Esperanto**."

"That's very curious," Alice thought. "But everything's curious
130 *today. I think I may as well go in at once."*

Now that you've glimpsed what I've glimpsed, what do you think? Is it possible that the comments of gaming's most passionate proponents are more than mere hyperbole[22] after all? Take the words of Jean-Francois Williams, author of *Williams Almanac: Everything*
135 *You Ever Wanted to Know About Video Games.*

He says, "We're at the beginning of a new art form." He calls interactive entertainment "a grand experiment," one bringing new storytelling elements to the culture. "We've been involved in passive entertainment forever," he adds. "Now, interactivity will be huge. Our
140 palette will be much broader,[23] and people will be able to be somebody [in the cyberworld] they could only dream of being otherwise."

It is still early in this revolution, too early perhaps to determine how the expansive opportunities in the cyberworld will carry into the real world. For all the experimentation and interactivity the
145 technology enables, for instance, it may also create expectations difficult to fulfill.

One teacher I know says she's seen children get frustrated quickly when faced with obstacles in the learning process that don't brush aside as quickly as they do in games. But, she adds, it's far too early to
150 add up all the pluses and minuses of interactive entertainment.

In more personal terms, it's still your choice whether to jump into this new world, approach cautiously, or, if it's not for you, stay in front of the TV or behind the cover of a good book.

But I think Alice had one point we can agree on. This wonderland
155 is only getting **"curiouser and curiouser!"**

About the Author

Gloria Goodale is arts and culture correspondent for the *Christian Science Monitor.*

---

[22] **more than mere hyperbole**   more than just deliberate exaggeration
[23] **our palette will be much broader**   the range of tools we will have to use will be wider

• **105**

After You Read

Understanding the Text

A. Multiple choice. For each item below, circle the **two** best answers.

1. The purpose of the article is to _____.

   a. analyze the story, *Through the Looking Glass* by Lewis Carroll

   b. persuade readers that electronic games can have positive value

   c. convince parents to share the gaming experience with their kids

   d. warn parents of the harmful effects of video games

2. From the first two paragraphs (page 101), we can infer that the author _____.

   a. is very enthusiastic about video games

   b. has been a fan of video games for a long time

   c. has a computer in her home

   d. does not know much about Lewis Carroll's books

3. The author believes that interactive video games have the power to change the way _____.

   a. children see themselves

   b. children think

   c. teachers teach

   d. animals behave

4. Two examples given by the author of how games can provide important lessons for life are _____.

   a. battling with enchanted creatures in "Magic"

   b. getting frustrated with obstacles in the learning process

   c. learning to care for pets

   d. learning how hard it is to be an adult

5. "Games are the new Esperanto" means that _____.

    a. games are now written in a new language called Esperanto

    b. games use ways of communicating that can be understood by everyone

    c. people in all parts of the world enjoy video games

    d. the language of video games is universal

B. Consider the issues. Work with a partner to answer the questions below.

1. Find these benefits of video gaming given in the article. Write the games that provide these benefits under **Example** in the chart below.

BENEFIT	EXAMPLE
Learning to care for other creatures	*"Seaman" by Sega*
Learning how hard it is to be an adult	_____
Learning to participate in a storytelling experience	_____
Learning to communicate with people in other parts of the world	_____

2. Choose one of the benefits in the chart. Do you agree or disagree that video games really provide this benefit? Explain your position to your partner.

Reading Skill

Following a story line

In a narrative, the writer tells a story from his or her own experience. Where there is a major shift in time or focus, the writer often provides clear signals to help readers follow the story. For example, in "Getting Into the Game," the author introduces characters from Lewis Carroll's stories as an amusing way to introduce new sections of the story.

"Tell me which way I ought to walk from here?" asked Alice. "That," the Cheshire Cat replied, "depends a good deal on where you want to get to."

On the story map below, draw arrows that show the direction of the events in the story. On the line between each section, write the first few words of the quotation used by the author to signal the shift.

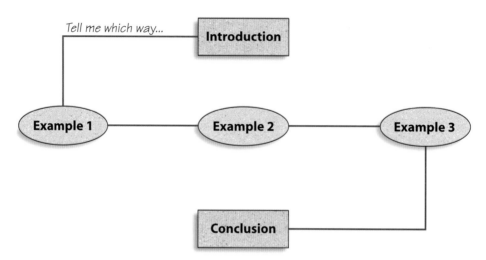

Tell me which way...

Introduction

Example 1 — Example 2 — Example 3

Conclusion

Building Vocabulary

Compound words

Compound words are created by combining two shorter words. Some of these words have hyphens that connect their component parts. You can usually figure out the meaning of a compound word by breaking it down into its simpler parts.

wonderland—a place filled with wonder; a fantasy land

The component parts of many compound words are separated by a hyphen:

late-bloomer—someone who excels at something late in life

cyber-pet—a pet that only exists in the world of computers and information systems

A. Underline the compound words in the following sentences. Then explain what each one means or provide a synonym. (Note: some sentences have more than one compound word.)

1. Ever since I started fumbling with joysticks and game controllers, I feel I've been falling slow-motion into a place I didn't really understand or appreciate.

2. This console game uses voice-recognition technology.

_____

3. We hatch a pea-sized egg that we have to lay in a watery tomb.

_____

4. It proves to be as strong-willed and demanding as any flesh-and-blood charge I've ever cared for.

_____

5. In that sense, it's also a game that departs from the linear concept of storytelling in place for several thousands of years of Western literature.

_____

6. She soon learns that even cyber-life isn't as easy to control as she'd like.

_____

B. The chart below has several examples of compound word groups. Try adding an example of your own to each group. Then give a sample phrase with your word on the right side of the chart.

low-risk	_____
medium-risk	_____
high-risk	a high-risk adventure
startled-looking	_____
strange-looking	_____
_____	_____
worldwide	_____
storewide	_____
_____	_____
16-year-old	_____
1-week-old	_____
_____	_____

Gerunds as complements

Gerunds are words that come from verbs but act like nouns. A gerund stands for the act of doing something. Gerund complements follow some verbs directly:

I enjoy *playing* video games.

Verbs that can be followed directly by gerunds include *appreciate, begin, continue, enjoy, finish, forget, hate, hear, like, love, prefer,* and *regret*.

Phrases with prepositions like *for, of, to,* and *from* often include a gerund.

We look forward to *seeing* you again soon.

I have just achieved the golden ring of *parenting*.

A. Some of the sentences below contain prepositional phrases with gerunds. If a sentence contains a prepositional phrase + gerund, draw brackets [ ] around the whole phrase. Note that not all words ending in -ing are gerunds (they may be continuous forms of verbs or modifiers).

1. It's the world that is coming, a world that is taking over the one in which you and I grew up. (no gerund)

2. This is a game in which the player has to make lots of decisions, each taking the story in a new direction.

3. By writing her own story, the player becomes author.

4. But the first thing he does is send an onscreen instant message, part of the game, to tell his new cyberspace opponent, ViperBat, that he is playing under his mother's name.

5. Williams says, "We're at the beginning of a new art form."

B. Answer the following questions using gerund complements.

1. What do you enjoy playing in your free time?

_____

2. Who do you like seeing when you get home?

_____

3. What would you like to finish doing as soon as you get the chance?

_____

1. Do you think that children should be encouraged to play video games. If yes, what kinds? If not, why not?

2. **Group work.** With a small group, imagine that you are entering a game world filled with fantastic creatures.

   a. each group member invent his or her avatar and give it a name

   b. describe the characters your avatar will meet in the game world

   c. describe at least one problem you will encounter and explain how you will overcome it.

3. Reread the author's final advice to her readers:

   In more personal terms, it's still your choice whether to jump into this new world, approach cautiously, or, if it's not for you, stay in front of the TV or behind the cover of a good book.

   Which choice do you think you will make? Write at least one paragraph explaining your choice.

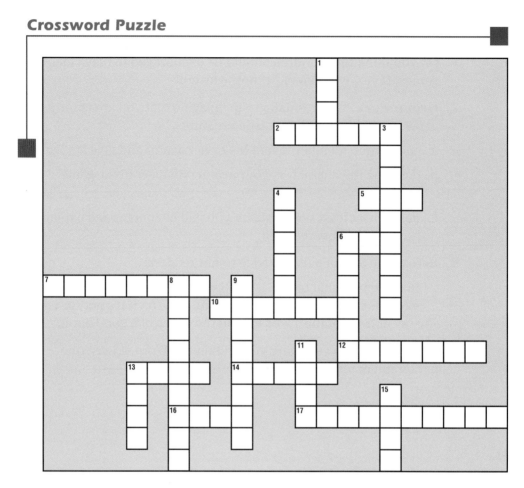

Use words from the reading to complete the crossword puzzle.

Across:

2 A fertilized, growing egg

5 An evil spell

6 Expression meaning "Now I understand!"

7 Device used to control movement on a screen

10 English author Lewis _____

12 Great mental suffering

13 Opposite of "fast"

14 Prefix meaning "between"

16 Company that created "Seaman"

17 *Alice in* _____

Down:

1 The golden _____ of parenting

3 A universal langage

4 Character with superhuman power

6 First name of a famous pilot

8 "Curiouser and _____"

9 A disadvantage in a game or contest

11 Sound made by cats

13 The _____, a popular electronic game

15 Dogs, cats, and fish for example

Chapter 10

Call of the Riled

Chapter Focus

The act of using technology to extend the human voice produces a particular result ... everyone becomes involved in what was meant to be a private conversation.

—*Marshall McLuhan*
Professor and writer
(1911–1980)

CONTENT:
Cell phone etiquette

READING SKILL:
Recognizing paragraph transitions

BUILDING VOCABULARY:
Synonyms and antonyms; using suffixes -*ful* and -*less*

LANGUAGE FOCUS:
Reduced relative clauses

Before You Read

1. Are cell phones common where you live? What do people use them for? Do you own a cell phone or other handheld communication device? How often do you use it?

2. Have you ever been in an embarrassing situation because of a cell phone? Describe what happened and explain why it was embarrassing.

3. Read the title of the article and then take one minute to skim the text. What do you think the article will be about? Share your ideas with a partner.

Reading Passage

CALL OF THE RILED[1]

by Kenneth Terrell and Sara Hammel

from *U.S. News and World Report*

1   During a performance last March of the **Broadway** play *The Lion in Winter*, an audience member's cell phone rang. After putting up with the annoyance for 20 seconds, actor **Laurence Fishburne** stopped the scene and boomed: "Will you turn off that phone,
5   please?" He got a rousing ovation.[2]

It has not yet risen to an **organized consumer movement**, but there are unmistakable signs of a backlash[3] against the 75 million handheld communications devices now on the American scene. More affordable and easier to use than ever, cell phones keep users in

---

[1] **riled**   very irritated; upset

[2] **rousing ovation**   prolonged, enthusiastic applause

[3] **backlash**   angry reaction

10 touch whether they are on the road, at the grocery store, or in the middle of a national park.

And therein lies the problem. For every businessman grateful for being able to close a deal in Los Angeles while lunching at a restaurant in New York, there is another patron who wishes he would shut up.
15 And for every commuter efficiently chatting with the home office while rolling down the interstate,[4] there is another motorist wishing he had one of those bumper stickers that says "Hang up and drive."

Driving danger. A cell phone conversation is not the same as a face-to-face one: It's often louder, for one thing, because people
20 mistakenly think they have to shout to be heard on the other end, and it's annoying for eavesdroppers[5] because it goes only one way. On the road, a cell phone conversation is downright[6] dangerous. According to a **University of Toronto** study, car phone users are four times as likely as other drivers to have an accident. "Cell phones have merged
25 everything into one all-purpose space," says Paul Levinson, a communications professor at **Fordham University** and author of *Digital McLuhan: A Guide to the **Information Millennium***. "There are no guideposts. We do what we want regardless of where we are." Now, however, as the liabilities of cell phone use start competing
30 with the benefits, society is instituting some rules of wireless behavior, both on and off the road.

Examples of boorish[7] cell phone conduct abound. At the Pillar House restaurant in Newton Falls, Massachusetts, in April, a cell phone owner wanted to avoid annoying the people at his own table,
35 so he turned to diners at an adjoining table and conversed loudly toward them. In a class for MBA[8] students in Milwaukee last month, a professor talked on his cell phone through much of a student presentation that counted for 20 percent of the student's grade.

Cell phone users seem to have no clue[9] how rude or careless they
40 can be. In a new survey by SBC Communications (whose brands include Cellular One and Pacific Bell), 53 percent of respondents gave other wireless phone users a C, a D, or an F for manners. Encouragingly, most found it inappropriate to use a wireless phone at a funeral (98 percent), a restaurant (86 percent), or a movie theater

---

[4] **interstate**   large, usually four-lane highway that crosses state lines
[5] **eavesdroppers**   people who listen to the private conversations of others
[6] **downright**   absolutely
[7] **boorish**   rude and insensitive
[8] **MBA**   Master of Business Administration degree
[9] **have no clue**   not understand; have no idea

45   (96 percent). Oddly, however, 83 percent of the respondents gave themselves an A or a B for cell phone manners.

      Many cell phone users are unapologetic about their habits. Kathy Posner, a public relations executive and self-described loud talker from Chicago, keeps one phone in her purse, another in her briefcase,
50   and two in her car. She sees nothing wrong with talking in a restaurant or on the train. Soon, however, she and her cell-phone-loving cohorts[10] may find themselves without a choice.

      Shush![11] The Hampton Jitney, a bus that shuttles thousands of **power brokers and beautiful people** from Manhattan to Long
55   Island's posh[12] eastern end, limits cell phone calls to three minutes each and allows them only when absolutely necessary. Offenders will be gently reminded. Tom Neely, vice president of marketing for the service, says the policy was instituted two years ago after customers said they didn't want to listen to other people's business or personal
60   affairs. "Cell phone users don't know how loud they are talking," Neely says.

      Loud talkers are an irritant to the restaurant industry as well, and many of the better restaurants are doing something about them. After numerous requests at the Pillar House, phones were banned from its
65   dining room. The St. Louis Club in Missouri allows cell phones only in its lobby; New York's Old Town Bar displays a picture of a cell phone with a red line through it; and several other upscale[13] Manhattan eateries, including trendy Union Square Cafe, prohibit phones in their dining rooms.

70   SBC Communications recently launched a campaign[14] to make proper cell phone etiquette as common as the phones themselves. In its April survey of wireless phone users, the company enlisted Peggy Post, great-granddaughter-in-law of manners maven[15] **Emily Post**, to interpret the results and offer solutions. Her simple guidelines: Don't
75   talk during lectures, concerts, plays, and movies; use a vibrating phone instead of a ringer; and keep your conversations very short.

      The penalty for cell phone use while driving can be bodily injury, not just missing a few minutes of a movie. "Everyone thinks they can handle talking on the cell phone, eating snacks, changing radio
80   stations, and driving a stick shift without having an accident," says

---

[10] **cohorts**   friends who share the same opinions and lifestyle

[11] **Shush!**   Be quiet!

[12] **posh**   smart; fashionable

[13] **upscale**   high class, expensive; intended for wealthy customers

[14] **launch a campaign**   start promoting an idea, new product, etc.

[15] **manners maven**   expert on the subject of proper social behavior

Julie Rochman of the Insurance Institute for Highway Safety. But, she says, "There's no doubt about it: It's going to increase your risk."

As a result, more communities are considering laws to limit the use of wireless phones behind the wheel. In March, a few weeks after a 85 phone-using driver crashed in front of the Brooklyn, Ohio, City Hall,[16] the Cleveland suburb passed a law making it illegal to use a cell phone while driving unless both hands are on the wheel.

Thirteen states are considering bills[17] that restrict the use of phones while driving. But only three—California, Florida, and 90 Massachusetts—have passed any laws, and none of those is outright prohibitive,[18] focusing on keeping one hand on the wheel and one ear free for traffic noises. The argument against such laws, says Matt Sundeen, a policy specialist at the National Conference of State Legislatures, is that "cell phones are part of people's lives now, and 95 that's too difficult to take away." Even those who approve of restrictions admit they are difficult to enforce: How do the cops prove you were using your cell phone when you caused that 10-car pileup? Critics of restrictions also point to the positive safety features of cell phones: Thousands of people each day use wireless phones to report 100 accidents and other incidents they witness from the road.

Trying to fend off legislation,[19] the wireless industry has mounted a driving-safety-awareness campaign. The **National Highway Traffic Safety Administration**, along with InsWeb.com (an insurance-information Web site), also offers road-related advice:

105 Keep your phone in easy reach so you can grab it without taking your eyes off the road.

Memorize the keypad and functions to make dialing easier.

Hang up in heavy traffic and in hazardous driving conditions.

And, when in doubt, remember the immortal words of Laurence 110 Fishburne.

[16] **City Hall**   building where government offices for the city are located
[17] **bills**   proposed laws
[18] **outright prohibitive**   preventing people from using something at all
[19] **fend off legislation**   stop or delay the passing of laws

After You Read

Understanding the Text

A. True, False, or Impossible to Know? Read the statements below and write T (True), F (False), or I (Impossible to Know).

_____ 1. At the performance described in the first paragraph, the audience reacted angrily to Laurence Fishburne's interruption of the play.

_____ 2. In many countries around the world, it is considered extremely impolite to use a cell phone in a restaurant.

_____ 3. Most people speak more loudly into cell phones than they do in ordinary face-to-face conversation.

_____ 4. Drivers using cell phones are more likely to have accidents than other drivers.

_____ 5. The professor who talked on his wireless phone while a student was giving a presentation is an example of extremely rude cell phone conduct.

_____ 6. In a survey by SBC Communications, 98 percent of the respondents felt it was OK to use a cell phone at a funeral.

_____ 7. New York City has established a law banning cell phones from all trains and other public transportation systems.

B. Consider the issues. Work with a partner to answer the questions below.

1. Why do you think the audience gave Laurence Fishburne a standing ovation? Would you have joined in if you had been there?

2. What are some of the advantages of handheld communication devices mentioned in the article? What are some disadvantages?

3. What type of legislation (line 101) do you think the wireless industry is trying to prevent? Why are they opposed to such laws? What are they doing instead?

Recognizing paragraph transitions

In a piece of writing made up of several paragraphs, writers use **transitions** to connect the paragraphs. A transition usually links the first sentence of a new paragraph with an idea or piece of information in the previous paragraph. Transitions between paragraphs may be in the form of a word or a phrase:

> As a result, more communities are considering laws to limit the use of wireless phones behind the wheel. (lines 83–84)

As a result is a transitional phrase that connects the main point of the previous paragraph (cell phones increase the risk of accidents) to the information given in the next (communities are considering laws).

Transitions may also be made by repeating or referring to an idea from the previous paragraph:

> And for every commuter efficiently chatting with the home office while rolling down the interstate, there is another motorist wishing he had one of those bumper stickers that says "Hang up and drive." (lines 15–17)

> *Driving* danger. A cell phone conversation is not the same as a face-to-face one...

(The first word in the paragraph, *driving*, refers back to the last word in the previous sentence by repeating the verb. Note, however, that in many cases the author may use a word with the same or similar meaning instead of repeating the exact word.)

Find each pair of phrases in the article and reread the two paragraphs they are from. Write the word or words the author uses to make a transition between the two paragraphs.

1. More affordable and easier to use...

   And therein lies...   (lines 8–12)   _____

2. Now, however, as the liabilities of cell phone use...

   Examples of boorish...   (lines 29–32)   _____

3. "Cell phone users don't know..."

   Loud talkers are an irritant...   (lines 60–63)   _____

Synonyms and antonyms

Synonyms are pairs of words that are similar in meaning. For example, *dangerous* and *hazardous* are synonyms.

Antonyms have opposite or nearly opposite meaning. Words like *easy* and *difficult* are antonyms.

A. Number the paragraphs in the article from 1 to 15. Then find the words below.

1. In paragraph 1, find a synonym for *drama*.

_____

2. In paragraph 1, find an antonym for *whispered*.

_____

3. In paragraph 2, which word means *certain*?

_____

4. In paragraph 3, find an antonym for *thankless*.

_____

5. In paragraph 3, find a phrasal verb (two words) that means *driving*.

_____

6. In paragraph 4, find a word that means the opposite of *correctly*.

_____

7. In paragraph 5, find an antonym for *polite*.

_____

8. In paragraph 8, find a synonym for *restrict*.

_____

9. In paragraph 10, find a synonym for *expert*.

_____

10. In paragraph 15, find a word that means *lasting forever*.

_____

A **suffix** is added to the end of a word to change its meaning or form. For example, the suffixes _-ful_ and _-less_ added to words changes them to adjectives with opposite meanings.

A _careful_ driver keeps both hands on the wheel.

Careless drivers can cause serious accidents.

B. Read the summary below. Underline all of the adjectives ending in -less or -ful. Work with a partner to find a definition or synonym for each of the underlined words.

There have been many signs in recent years that Americans are becoming increasingly upset with the unrestricted use of cell phones, especially in public places. Although handheld communication devices can be wonderful in emergency situations, it is the thoughtless way many people use them that is causing the uproar. For example, some cell phone lovers don't think twice about carrying on loud conversations on buses and trains, regardless of what their fellow passengers think. On the road, drivers who use cell phones are not as watchful as motorists who keep their hands on the wheel. In some states, laws are being proposed that restrict the use of cell phones on the road. Some private establishments are asking customers to be more respectful of others by turning their cell phones off. While some customers may react angrily to this new rule, others are sure to be thankful that they won't have to eavesdrop on their neighbors' conversations.

Reduced relative clauses

A **relative clause** tells more about the noun it follows. A relative clause is introduced with *who, that, which,* or *whose.*

> For every businessman with a cell phone, there is another patron *who wishes he would shut up.*

> A professor talked on his cell phone through much of a student presentation *that counted for 20 percent of the student's grade.*

To make writing more efficient, we can reduce some relative clauses by omitting the introductory word and adding *-ing* to the verb.

> The town passed a law *which made* it illegal to use a cell phone while driving.

> The town passed a law *making* it illegal to use a cell phone while driving.

A. Find the relative clause in each of the following sentences. Reduce the clause by crossing out any words you can delete and making any other changes as necessary.

1. For every driver with a cell phone, there is another motorist
wishing
who wishes all handheld communication devices were illegal.

2. Loud cell phone conversations are especially annoying for tired commuters who just hope to have a quiet ride home.

3. Thirteen states are considering bills that restrict the use of phones while driving.

B. Complete these sentences with reduced relative clauses of your own.

1. I'm tired of people (talk) _____

2. There should be a law (prohibit) _____

3. The authors give several examples of rude wireless behavior, (include) _____

1. Where do you think the use of cell phones and other handheld communication devices should be allowed? Where do you think they should be restricted? Why?

2. The chart below lists several places where people might be disturbed by the use of cell phones. With a partner, decide on one reason why cell phone use might annoy other people in these locations. In the column on the right, give at least one suggestion for a rule cell phone users should follow in each place.

Restaurant	*Upsets digestion*	*Turn it off*
Classroom		
Train or bus		
Library		
Department store		
Church or temple		

3. With your partner, imagine that you are in charge of one of the establishments listed above. How would you inform people of your decision to prohibit or limit the use of cell phones? Choose one of the following and write it on another piece of paper.

   a. Write a letter to the regular patrons or customers explaining the new rule.

   b. Design an announcement or sign to remind people of what they can and cannot do.

Crossword Puzzle

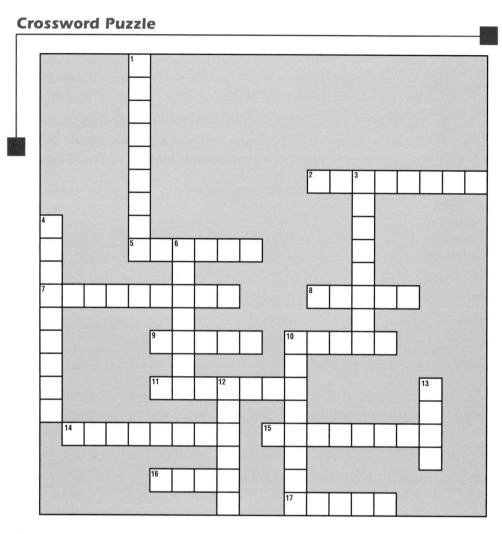

Use words from the reading to complete the crossword puzzle.

Across:

2 Angry reaction
5 Residential area near a city
7 Very dangerous
8 Message to cell phone users in cars: "Hang up and _____."
9 Proposed laws
10 Part of a play
11 And _____ lies the problem.
14 Without wires
15 Words with opposite meanings
16 To close a _____
17 Be quiet!

Down:

1 People who buy things and use them
3 Launch a _____
4 Actor Laurence _____
6 Rude and insensitive
10 Words with the same or similar meanings
12 As a _____, ...
13 Very fashionable, upscale

Chapter ▲ **11** The Art of Reading

There is no frigate[1]
*   like a book*
To take us lands
*   away*
Nor any coursers[2] like
*   a page*
Of prancing poetry.

—*Emily Dickenson*
Poet
(1830–1886)

Chapter Focus

CONTENT:
Suggestions for becoming a skillful reader

READING SKILL:
Recognizing analogies

BUILDING VOCABULARY:
Word forms

LANGUAGE FOCUS:
Expressing similarity and difference

---

[1] **frigate**   a kind of ship

[2] **coursers**   an old word for horses

Before You Read

1. When did you learn to read? How did you learn? When did you begin to enjoy it? What is your favorite place and time for reading? Who are your favorite authors?

2. Scan the first paragraph of the article (pages 126–127) and circle the names of the people mentioned. Who are they? What do they have in common?

3. Who do you look to for advice on living? What books do you think are important for everyone to read in order to become an educated person in today's world?

Reading Passage

THE ART OF READING

by Lin Yu T'ang

from *The Importance of Understanding*

1   Reading or the enjoyment of books has always been regarded among the charms of a cultured life and is respected and envied by those who rarely give themselves that privilege. This is easy to understand when we compare the difference between the life of **a**
5   **man who does no reading** and that of a man who does. The man who has not[3] the habit of reading is imprisoned in his immediate world, in respect to time and space. His life falls into a set routine; he is limited to contact and conversation with a few friends and acquaintances, and he sees only what happens in his immediate neighborhood. From this
10   prison there is no escape. But the moment he takes up a book, he

---

[3] **the man who has not**   the person who does not have

immediately enters a different world, and if it is a good book, he is immediately put in touch with one of the best talkers of the world. This talker leads him on and carries him into a different country or a different age, or unburdens to him some of his personal regrets, or
15 discusses with him some special line or aspect of life that the reader knows nothing about. An ancient author puts him in communion with a dead spirit of long ago, and as he reads along, he begins to imagine what that ancient author looked like and what type of person he was. Both **Mencius** and **Ssuma Ch'ien**, China's greatest historian, have
20 expressed the same idea. Now to be able to live two hours out of twelve in a different world and take one's thoughts off the claims of the immediate present is, of course, a privilege to be envied by people shut up in their bodily prison. Such a change of environment is really similar to travel in its psychological effect.

25   But there is more to it than this. The reader is always carried away into a world of thought and reflection. Even if it is a book about physical events, there is a difference between seeing such events in person or living through them, and reading about them in books, for then the events always assume the quality of the spectacle[4] and the
30 reader becomes a detached spectator. The best reading is therefore that which leads us into this contemplative mood,[5] and not that which is merely occupied with the report of events. The tremendous amount of time spent on newspapers I regard as not reading at all, for the average readers of papers are mainly concerned with getting
35 reports about events and happenings without contemplative value.

The best formula for the object of reading, in my opinion, was stated by Huang Shanku, a **Sung poet** and friend of **Su Tungp'o**. He said, "A scholar who hasn't read anything for three days feels that his talk has no flavor (becomes insipid[6]), and his own face becomes
40 hateful to look at (in the mirror)." What he means, of course, is that reading gives a man a certain charm and flavor, which is the entire object of reading, and only reading with this object can be called an art. One doesn't read to "improve one's mind," because when one begins to think of improving his mind, all the pleasure of reading is
45 gone. He is the type of person who says to himself. "I must read Shakespeare, and I must read **Sophocles**, and I must read the entire **Five-foot Shelf of Dr. Eliot**, so I can become an educated man." I'm sure that man will never become educated. He will force himself one evening to read Shakespeare's *Hamlet* and come away, as if from a
50 bad dream, with no greater benefit than that he is able to say that he

---

[4] **spectacle** an impressive display

[5] **contemplative mood** calm and thoughtful state of mind

[6] **insipid** dull; not interesting

had "read" *Hamlet.* Anyone who reads a book with a sense of obligation does not understand the art of reading. This type of reading with a business purpose is in no way different from a senator's reading up on files and reports before he makes a speech. It 55 is asking for business advice and information, and not reading at all.

Reading for the cultivation of personal charm of appearance and flavor in a speech is then, according to Huang, the only admissible kind of reading. This charm of appearance must evidently be interpreted as something other than physical beauty. What Huang 60 means by "hateful to look at" is not physical ugliness. There are ugly faces that have a fascinating charm and beautiful faces that are insipid to look at. I have among my Chinese friends one whose head is shaped like a bomb and yet who is nevertheless always a pleasure to see. The most beautiful face among Western authors, so far as I 65 have seen them in pictures, was that of **G.K. Chesterton**. There was such a diabolical conglomeration[7] of mustache, glasses, fairly bushy eyebrows and knitted lines where the eyebrows met. One felt there were a vast number of ideas playing about inside that forehead, ready at any time to burst out from those quizzically penetrating eyes. That 70 is what Huang would call a beautiful face, a face not made up by powder and rouge, but by the sheer force of thinking. As for flavor of speech, it all depends on one's way of reading. Whether one has "flavor" or not in his talk, depends on his method of reading. If a reader gets the flavor of books, he will show that flavor in his 75 conversations, and if he has flavor in his conversations, he cannot help also having a flavor in his writing.

Hence I consider flavor or taste as the key to all reading. It necessarily follows that taste is selective and individual, like the taste for food. The most hygienic[8] way of eating is, after all, eating what 80 one likes, for then one is sure of his digestion. In reading as in eating, what is one man's meat may be another's poison.[9] A teacher cannot force his pupils to like what he likes in reading, and a parent cannot expect his children to have the same tastes as himself.

There can be, therefore, no books that one absolutely must read. 85 For our intellectual interests grow like a tree or flow like a river. So long as there is proper sap,[10] the tree will grow anyhow, and so long as there is fresh current from the spring, the water will flow. When

---

[7] **diabolical conglomeration**   devilish, ugly, or evil-looking combination

[8] **hygienic**   clean; free from disease

[9] **what is one man's meat may be another man's poison**   what is good for one person may be bad for another

[10] **sap**   a liquid inside a plant that carries nutrients to its parts

water strikes a granite cliff, it just goes around it; when it finds itself
in a pleasant low valley, it stops and meanders there a while; when it
90 finds itself in a deep mountain pond, it is content to stay there; when
it finds itself traveling over rapids, it hurries forward. Thus, without
any effort or determined aim, it is sure of reaching the sea some day.

I regard the discovery of one's favorite author as the most critical
event[11] in one's intellectual development. There is such a thing as the
95 affinity[12] of spirits, and among the authors of ancient and modern
times, one must try to find an author whose spirit is akin with his
own. Only in this way can one get any real good out of reading. One
has to be independent and search out his masters. Who is one's
favorite author, no one can tell, probably not even the man himself. It
100 is like love at first sight. The reader cannot be told to love this one or
that one, but when he has found the author he loves, he knows it
himself by a kind of instinct. We have such famous cases of
discoveries of authors. Scholars seem to have lived in different ages,
separated by centuries, and yet their modes of thinking and feeling
105 were so akin that their coming together across the pages of a book
was like a person finding his own image. **George Eliot** described her
first reading of **Rousseau** as an electric shock. **Nietzsche** felt the
same thing about **Schopenhauer**, but Schopenhauer was a peevish[13]
master and Nietzsche was a violent-tempered pupil, and it was
110 natural that the pupil later rebelled against the teacher.

It is only this kind of reading, this discovery of one's favorite
author, that will do one any good at all. Like a man falling in love with
his sweetheart at first sight, everything is right. She is of the right
height, has the right face, the right color of hair, the right quality of
115 voice and the right way of speaking and smiling. This author is not
something that a young man needs to be told about by his teacher.
The author is just right for him; his style, his taste, his point of view,
his mode of thinking, are all right. And then the reader proceeds to
devour[14] every word and every line that the author writes, and
120 because there is a spiritual affinity he absorbs and readily digests
everything. The author has cast a spell[15] over him, and he is glad to be
under the spell, and in time his own voice and manner and way of
smiling and way of talking become like the author's own. Thus he
truly steeps himself in his literary lover and derives from these books

---

[11] **critical event**   most important thing that can happen; a turning point
[12] **affinity**   natural liking or attraction
[13] **peevish**   bad-tempered; irritable
[14] **devour**   read eagerly
[15] **cast a spell**   used magic to influence him

125   sustenance[16] for his soul. After a few years, the spell is over and he grows a little tired of this lover and seeks for new literary lovers, and after he has had three or four lovers and completely eaten them up, he emerges as an author himself. There are many readers who never fall in love, like many young men and women who flirt around and are

130   incapable of forming a deep attachment to a particular person. They can read any and all authors, and they never amount to anything.

     Such a conception of the art of reading completely precludes[17] the idea of reading as a duty or as an obligation. In China, one often encourages students to "study bitterly." There was a famous scholar

135   who studied bitterly and who stuck an awl[18] in his calf when he fell asleep while studying at night. There was another scholar who had a maid stand by his side as he was studying at night, to wake him up every time he fell asleep. This was nonsensical. If one has a book lying before him and falls asleep while some wise ancient author is

140   talking to him, he should just go to bed. No amount of sticking an awl in his calf or of shaking him up by a maid will do him any good. Such a man has lost all sense of pleasure of reading. Scholars who are worth anything at all never know what is called "a hard grind" or what "bitter study" means. They merely love books and read on

145   because they cannot help themselves.

     What, then, is the true art of reading? The simple answer is to just take up a book and read when the mood comes. To be thoroughly enjoyed, reading must be entirely spontaneous.

About the Author

Lin Yu-T'ang (1895–1976) was born in China but received much of his education in the West—at Harvard University and at the University of Leipzig. He was a respected professor at Peking National University for many years, and later was the chancellor of Nanyang University in Singapore. A writer of novels as well as nonfiction, he is known for pieces which explain modern China to readers from other cultures.

---

[16] **sustenance**   something, especially food, that supports life

[17] **precludes**   prevents something from happening

[18] **awl**   tool with a sharp point for punching holes in leather

After You Read

Understanding the Text

A. Identify the author's advice. Which of the following advice does the author give about reading? Check (√) your answers.

_____ **1.** Travel to different countries and learn new languages.

_____ **2.** Read mainly to improve your mind.

_____ **3.** Read mainly for the pleasure of reading.

_____ **4.** Cultivate friendships with literary lovers.

_____ **5.** Begin with great books like the Bible and the *Book of Changes*.

_____ **6.** Search for your own favorite authors.

_____ **7.** Study hard every night.

_____ **8.** Punish yourself if you fall asleep while reading.

_____ **9.** Take up a book and read when you are in the mood.

B. Consider the issues. Work with a partner to answer the questions below.

1. In the author's view, a person who is not in the habit of reading is like a person in prison (lines 5–7). What kind of prison does he mean? Do you agree or disagree?

2. Reread the second paragraph (lines 25–35). Why does the author prefer books to newspapers? Why does he regard reading newspapers as a waste of time?

3. In lines 93–110, the author advises readers to "fall in love" with an author and gives several examples. What does he mean by this? Do you think you will take his advice?

> ### Recognizing analogies
> An **analogy** is a comparison between two things that are similar in some respects but different in others. Writers often use analogies to help explain something in an interesting or entertaining way.
>
> **Example:**
> Our intellectual interests grow like a tree or flow like a river. So long as there is proper sap, the tree will grow anyhow, and so long as there is fresh current from the spring, the water will flow.
>
> (The way intellectual interests grow is compared to the way trees grow and the way rivers flow.)
>
> By making this analogy, the author suggests that intellectual growth is a natural occurrence rather than something forced or mechanical.

The analogies below are from the reading. Below each selection, identify what two things or activities are being compared and explain how they are similar.

1. Now to be able to live two hours out of twelve in a different world and take one's thoughts off the claims of the immediate present is, of course, a privilege to be envied by people shut up in their bodily prison. Such a change of environment is really similar to travel in its psychological effect.

   reading: _travel_____ _____ because _they both take us away_

   from the place and time we are in now

2. It necessarily follows that taste is selective and individual, like the taste for food. The most hygienic way of eating is, after all, eating what one likes, for then one is sure of his digestion.

   taste for reading: _____ because _____

   _____

   _____

3. It is only this kind of reading, this discovery of one's favorite author, that will do one any good at all. Like a man falling in love with his sweetheart at first sight, everything is right.

   finding one's favorite author: _____ because

   _____

   _____

Building Vocabulary

Word forms
When you learn a new word, it's useful to learn other forms of the same word. You can find these forms in a dictionary.

A. Complete the chart below by adding the missing word forms. In some cases, there are two noun forms. Then check your ideas by looking in a dictionary.

NOUN	VERB	ADJECTIVE	ADVERB
1. history, historian	X	_____	_____
2. _____	envy	_____	enviably
3. immediacy	X	_____	_____
4. _____ _____	X	psychological	_____
5. spectacle	_____	spectacular	_____
6. _____ _____	inform	_____	informatively
7. _____	cultivate	_____	X
8. _____ _____	quiz	quizzical	_____

B. Choose words from the chart above to complete these sentences. More than one answer may be possible.

1. The author admired G.K. Chesterson's _____ eyes.

2. When a person falls in love, he or she knows it _____.

3. The _____ of good reading habits can take a lifetime.

4. Reading for _____, in the author's view, is not as worthwhile as reading for pleasure.

Expressing similarity and difference

Like or *as* can be used to show that one thing is similar to another.

> Taste is selective and individual, *like* the taste for food.

> The art of reading can be regarded *as* a conversation between author and reader.

(Note: In general, when used for this purpose, *as* is more formal than *like*.)

Different from or *the difference between* show that two things are not the same or similar. Statements of this type often include a clause that explains how the two things are different.

> Books are *different from* newspapers in that they cause the reader to contemplate events, not just get reports about them.

What can some people or ideas be compared to? How are some things different? Complete the following sentences with ideas of your own.

1. The difference between a person who reads and one who doesn't

   is that _____

2. Authors of great books are like _____

3. Newspapers are different from books in that _____

   _____

4. When reading a history book, the reader sees events in the past as

   _____

5. Reading for self-improvement is different from the art of reading

   in that _____

1. According to the author, the object of reading is to give a person "a certain charm and flavor." To achieve this goal, the author believes that it is more important to read for pleasure than it is to study hard. Do you agree or disagree? Discuss your ideas with a partner or a small group of your classmates.

2. Identify one of your own favorite authors. Find the following information about your choice and share it with a group of your classmates. If possible, bring a piece of the writer's work to show the group.

Dates of birth and death	_____
Country of origin	_____
Major works	_____
	_____
	_____
	_____
One other interesting fact	_____

3. Use the information in the chart to write a paragraph about your favorite author. Try to convince the reader that he or she really should get to know your "literary lover."

Crossword Puzzle

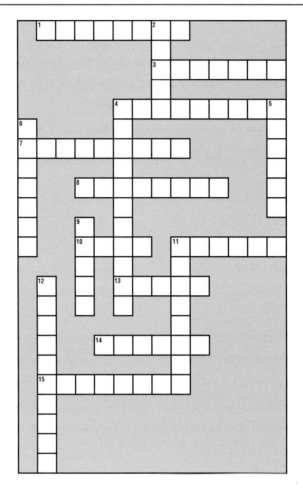

Use words from the reading to complete the crossword puzzle.

Across:

1 Natural liking or attraction

3 Someone who studies hard and is eager to learn

4 One who watches or observes

7 Place to find reports of daily events

8 To prevent something from happening

10 A writer of poems

11 One man's meat, another man's _____

13 Grow like a tree, flow like a _____

14 To read eagerly with great enthusiasm

15 Adjective form of *envy*

Down:

2 The key to all reading: flavor or _____

4 Author of *Hamlet*

5 Fast-moving water

6 Dull or uninteresting

9 To cast a _____

11 The most important reason for reading something

12 Western author with a beautiful face: G.K. _____

Chapter ▲ 12 When E.T. Calls

Arecibo Radio Telescope, Puerto Rico

The most beautiful thing we can experience is the mysterious. It is the source of all true art and science.

—Albert Einstein
Physicist
(1879–1955)

Chapter Focus

CONTENT:
Exploring the possibility of extraterrestrial life

READING SKILL:
Recognizing scenarios

BUILDING VOCABULARY:
Nouns derived from adjectives

LANGUAGE FOCUS:
Future perfect

Before You Read

1. Do you believe that intelligent life exists on other planets? If "yes," do you think trying to communicate with the extraterrestrials (E.T.) is worthwhile? Why or why not?

2. Read the title of the article and then take one minute to skim the text. What do you think the article will be about? Share your ideas with a partner.

3. If intelligent beings exist on other planets, what do you think they might look like? How would they communicate with us?

Reading Passage

WHEN E.T. CALLS

by Seth Shostak

from *Sharing the Universe*

1   If it happens, it will begin slowly and without warning in a radio telescope's cramped, cluttered control room. Here, under a hundred tons of steel faced off against the pinpoint gleams of the night sky, a back-burner experiment[1] could change the world.

5   We can imagine this future drama. The protagonist[2] is a lone astronomer, one of the two dozen or so who have gambled their careers on **SETI**. For weeks, she has been spending long nights seated in front of a bank of computer displays, nursing a cup of

---

[1] **back-burner experiment**   an experiment that is not considered very important

[2] **protagonist**   the central character

coffee[3] and intermittently[4] scribbling routine entries into a logbook.
10   On the screens, blocks of slowly changing text monitor the
electronics that are sifting through the thick cosmic static[5] collected
by the telescope. She sips at her drink and scans the displays'
laconic[6] reports. There is no theatrical music, no high-tech sound
effects; only the constant drone of fans in the electronics racks and
15   the faint, distant grind of the telescope's tracking motor. This is not
SETI as depicted by **Hollywood**. No control room loudspeaker will
suddenly break into a squeal or a rhythmic boom. There was a time,
many years earlier, when listening for audible signals was practical.
But modern SETI experiments monitor tens of millions of channels
20   simultaneously. Computers do the listening.

With only a soft beep as herald, the computers have found that one
channel in this multitude bears the hallmarks of extraterrestrial
origin.[7]

On the screen, a single line of text tells the tale, a string of numbers
25   giving the signal strength and exact frequency, terminated by the
cryptic words, "confirmed by FUDD." The FUDD, or Follow Up
Detection Device, is a specialized piece of electronics that orchestrates
a two-telescope procedure to confirm that a signal is coming from deep
space. The astronomer, while taking note, is not excited. After all, the
30   system finds such candidate signals five or six times a week. So far, all
have been traced to some sort of satellite interference or other man-
made source. None has been extraterrestrial.

Without prompting, the observing software swings the telescope
two degrees away from the targeted star system. Ten minutes go by
35   while the receivers accumulate more data. The FUDD then reports
that the signal has disappeared, as would be expected if it came from
the star itself. The astronomer pays close attention, but her blood
pressure doesn't change. It's probably another satellite, briefly
mimicking E.T. as it parades across the sky.

40   The telescope slews back[8] on target. Another ten minutes drag by,
and the FUDD reports that the signal has returned. The astronomer
puts her coffee down. Her eyes fix upon the display screen. The
telescope begins its cycle of on-off observations anew, and the

---

[3] **nursing a cup of coffee**   sipping at a cup of coffee very slowly

[4] **intermittently**   from time to time

[5] **thick cosmic static**   electronic noise from space

[6] **laconic**   very brief

[7] **bears the hallmarks of extraterrestrial origin**   shows signs of
coming from another planet

[8] **slews back**   turns sharply

evidence that this signal is extraterrestrial persists. She is now the
45   first witness to a staggering[9] sequence of events, a sequence that has
never before occurred. Within hours, she will call another radio
observatory to enlist its help. A detection at a distant telescope, by
other people and other equipment, will rule out fiendish
interference,[10] a bug in the system, or an ingenious college prank.
50   Within a few days, the signal will have been confirmed beyond
reasonable doubt. The drama begun by a computer's soft beep will
have grown to a worldwide din. We will finally have observational
proof that other thinking beings populate the Galaxy.[11]

Society's Reaction

55   If SETI scientists find a signal, some people will challenge the
detection, claiming that it's a hoax. After all, there are several million
people who still doubt astronauts ever walked on the moon. But the
reality of the result will be firmly based. Unlike the incessant claims
that **UFOs** are alien spacecraft, belief in a SETI success won't depend
60   on anecdotal evidence[12] or shaky, amateur videos. Anyone with
access to a suitable radio antenna would be able to confirm the signal
for himself, with his own equipment. There would be no doubt of its
legitimacy, and a SETI discovery would immediately precipitate
intense scientific inquiry. Every major telescope would be cranked in
65   the direction of E.T.'s signal, in the hope of learning more. But would
the discovery also provoke a dramatic response from society at
large? Would there be panic? Disbelief? A sudden eruption of
brotherly love and international goodwill?

Panic in the streets is unlikely. To be sure, **Orson Welles'** 1938
70   broadcast of *The War of the Worlds* did cause a certain amount of
alarm. But it's far less threatening to read of a signal from a distant
star system than to hear that aliens are afoot here on Earth.

A better example of the immediate reaction to the news that aliens
exist is the public's response to the August 1996 announcement by
75   **NASA** scientists that fossilized Martian microbes had been chipped
out of a meteorite. This was, after all, "life in space," even if it was
very small and long dead. It was later acclaimed as the biggest
science news story of the year, and yet it hardly affected anyone's
daily routine. The announcement generated one week of headlines,
80   after which the discovery dropped off the public's radar screen.

---

[9] **staggering**   amazing; awesome
[10] **fiendish interference**   obstruction with the intention to do harm
[11] **populate the Galaxy**   live on planets in the Milky Way Galaxy
[12] **anecdotal evidence**   proof based on individual reports and stories

No matter how anemic[13] the short-term reaction, most pundits[14] assume that the long-term consequences of finding extraterrestrials will be profound.

Alien Message

85 Out of the inevitable chaos following a SETI discovery, the facts of the detection would soon emerge—at least for those who are interested in facts. In view of the known technological limitations of SETI experiments, one can dare to predict what we would learn in those first, exciting days.

90 To begin with, where is the signal coming from? This might sound as if the answer should be obvious, but it won't be. For SETI searches that scan the heavens, the astronomers who first tune in E.T. will only know that the signal originates from a particular patch of sky. Many star systems could be camped out in such a patch. Fortunately, 95 uncertainty about the source of the signal could be quickly dispelled. Observations with a massively large instrument, such as the 1,000-foot **Arecibo dish**, could substantially narrow the piece of sky from which the transmission originates. A large constellation of telescopes, such as the **Very Large Array** in **New Mexico** (where 100 Ellie Arroway first heard the aliens in the movie ***Contact***), could zoom in more precisely on the spot where E.T. is broadcasting.

So within weeks of the discovery, we would likely know a few astronomical facts about E.T.'s home turf. But such information would be, at least in the public's mind, secondary. First and foremost, 105 the world will hanker to know what the aliens have to say. After all, the phone has rung, so what's the message?

Deciphering a message could take a long time. Indeed, it could take forever. As we've mentioned before, any signal we're likely to detect will come from a civilization that is enormously more 110 advanced than we. The aliens' message might be impossible to unravel. Imagine **Aristotle's** puzzlement if he were faced with the task of decoding a modern color-television signal. And Aristotle was no dummy.

In this case, or in the case that the signal turns out to be merely 115 intercepted alien radar devoid of *any* message, we still won't be left empty-handed. We will have proof, after all, of celestial company;[15] we will know that intelligent beings exist. We just won't know much about their particulars.

---

[13] **anemic**   weak; feeble

[14] **pundits**   experts in the field

[15] **proof of celestial company**   evidence that other intelligent beings exist in the universe

A more interesting scenario is that they might try to help us. A
120   deliberate transmission might be *designed* for infant technologies
such as our own. In that case the alien senders might take pity on our
cryptographers[16] by sending simple directions for deciphering their
broadcast, a kind of interspecies primer.[17] Elementary mathematics
is frequently suggested as a good first lesson. Indeed, the initial
125   messages received in the movie *Contact* amounted to a bit of boring
algebra. On the other hand, E.T. may figure that anyone able to
eavesdrop on his signals will probably have already taken algebra,
and send us pictures instead.

Given enough time and patience on the part of our extraterrestrial
130   tutors, there's no certain limit to what they could teach us.
Consequently, if we can crack the code of an alien signal, with or
without E.T.'s help, the impact on earthly society could be profound.
We would be in touch with an ancient and sophisticated culture. We
might skip eons of history[18] and leap into what otherwise would be a
135   far distant future.

Some consequences of this sort of contact are obvious. We could
bone up on[19] physics, chemistry, and astronomy. The aliens might fill
us in on how to get along. Perhaps they would even be considerate
enough to divulge the cure for death (a good thing to know from the
140   individual's point of view, although a real challenge for society).
There would be cause for optimism on Earth, for if E.T.'s society
could endure for countless centuries without self-destructing, then
presumably ours can as well.

About the Author

Seth Shostak is a scientist, teacher, and film producer. He has
degrees from Princeton University and the California Institute of
Technology. For much of his career, he conducted radio astronomy
research on galaxies, and has published approximately 50 papers in
professional journals. He has also produced many popular science
films. His book, *Sharing the Universe*, was published in 1998.

---

[16] **cryptographer** a person who figures out what codes mean

[17] **interspecies primer** an introductory set of instructions on how to
communicate with another species

[18] **eons of history** periods of time too long to measure

[19] **bone up on** study again after a long period of time; review

After You Read

Understanding the Text

A. **True or False?** Read the statements below and write T (True) or F (False). Correct the false statements.

   F   **1.** The author predicts that the first alien contact will ^{not} be very dramatic.

_____ **2.** Computers now monitor signals from space because the telescopes receive too many channels for humans to be able to hear.

_____ **3.** In the author's view, it is possible that civilizations on other planets are trying to make contact with people on Earth.

_____ **4.** So far, none of the signals received from space has been positively identified as an authentic communication from another planet.

_____ **5.** If a signal is "confirmed by FUDD," it is definitely recognized by scientists as a communication from outer space.

_____ **6.** There is hard scientific evidence that UFOs are alien spacecraft.

_____ **7.** The discovery of fossilized Martian microbes proves that intelligent life exists on other planets.

_____ **8.** Once a signal from outer space is detected, it will probably be easy for scientists to figure out where it is coming from and what it means.

_____ **9.** In general, Dr. Shostak thinks that making contact with intelligent life on other planets would have positive effects on human civilizations.

_____ **10.** From the tone of the writing, it is reasonable to assume that the author intended this book mainly for the general public.

B. Consider the issues. Work with a partner to answer the questions below.

1. Of the following statements, which is the most important argument for trying to detect signals from outer space? Discuss your choice with a partner.

   a. The discovery would interest more young people in mathematics and science.

   b. Beings from an advanced civilization could teach us how to get along.

   c. The aliens might teach us a cure for death.

2. Think of a good reason why scientists should NOT search for signals from outer space. What do you think Dr. Shostak's reply to this argument would be?

Reading Skill

Recognizing scenarios

A **scenario** describes an imaginary sequence of events. Writers sometimes use scenarios as a dramatic way of presenting what might happen. Scenarios are usually written in the simple present tense. This makes readers feel as if they are actually there, observing the action. As in a real story, time and place connectors link ideas and events to each other in order to construct a clear picture in the reader's mind.

A. Reread the scenario (lines 5–53) in the reading. Complete the following information.

Time: _the present_____

Place: _____

Main character: _____

Main events: **1.** _a computer detects a signal_____

              2. _____

              3. _____

              4. _____

              5. _____

B. Imagine your own scenario describing the first meeting between a human and a visitor from outer space. Describe your scenario to a partner.

Time: _____

Place: _____

Main character: _____

Main events:
1. _____
2. _____
3. _____
4. _____
5. _____

Building Vocabulary

Nouns derived from adjectives

Many adjectives can also be used as nouns without changing form. These nouns may be singular or plural.

We don't know if *extraterrestrial* life exists. (adjective)

No scientist has ever met an *extraterrestrial*. (singular noun)

Some nouns derived from adjectives function as collective nouns that stand for groups of people. These do not have singular forms and are preceded by *the*.

The response from *the public* might be panic in the streets.

A. Identify the **boldfaced** words in the following sentences as adjectives or nouns.

1. On the screens, blocks of slowly changing text monitor the
   noun
   electronics that are sifting through the thick cosmic static
   collected by the telescope.

2. There is no theatrical music, no **high-tech** sound effects; only
   the constant drone of fans in the **electronics** racks and the faint,
   distant grind of the telescope's tracking monitor.

3. If **extraterrestrials** exist, they are almost certainly not **human** beings.

4. Thousands of people claim to have seen **alien** spacecraft and some even say they have spoken with **aliens** face-to-face.

5. After all, the system finds such **candidate** signals five or six times a week.

6. We just won't know much about their **particulars.**

B. Many of the nouns that refer to the place of origin or nationality of people are derived from adjectives. Review the information below. Then complete the passage with the correct form of a word from the box.

singular or plural forms	collective (<u>the</u> + plural form only)
Asian(s)	the Chinese
European(s)	the Japanese
African(s)	the English
American(s)	the Sudanese
Australian(s)	the Irish
Iraqi(s)	the French
Korean(s)	the Dutch

Note: Nouns that name languages (French, English, Japanese) are often the same as the collective nouns for nationalities, but do not take the article "the," for example: I don't speak French.

If a team of technologically advanced extraterrestrial scientists visited our world today, they would probably find things very confusing. For example, they would be surprised to see so many different peoples from different nations speaking different languages. On their world, there is only one civilization and everyone speaks the same language.

We might try to explain to them that (1) <u>the French</u> live in France and speak (2) _____, and that (3) _____ live in China and speak (4) _____. That would be OK. But how can we explain that (5) _____ live in the Netherlands, which is also called Holland, and speak Dutch? Or that (6) _____ live in America and speak (7) _____? We could point out that both Iraqis and (8) _____ speak Arabic, but by that time our advanced extraterrestrials might decide to give up and go home.

Language Focus

Future perfect
Form:
   active: *will have* + past participle

   passive: *will have been* + past participle

Meaning: The **future perfect** form of a verb shows the relationship of a future event to a later time or event.
   The drama begun by a computer's soft beep *will have grown* to a worldwide din.

   Within a few days, the signal *will have been confirmed* beyond a reasonable doubt.

A. Complete the paragraph below with the future perfect form of each verb in parentheses.

By the time we are able to decode the first confirmed alien message, it's possible that we _____ (receive) many more signals from intelligent beings elsewhere in the universe. It also reasonable to assume that we _____ (advance) technologically ourselves. Whether we _____ (endure) without destroying each other is another question.

B. Imagine yourself ten years from now. What do you think will have happened? Compare your answers with a partner's.

1. What important things will you have accomplished?

   _____

2. How many new places will you have traveled to?

   _____

3. What new experiences will you have had?

   _____

4. What else do you think will have happened?

   _____

Discussion & Writing

1. Imagine that SETI astronomers have received signals from outer space. The signals have been confirmed, and the evidence is beyond doubt. The communication is from a technologically advanced and peaceful civilization that has evolved on a planet in the Milky Way Galaxy. How might this event change things on Earth? Discuss the possibilities with a partner or small group of your classmates.

2. **Group work.** Work with a small group of your classmates. Follow the steps below to discuss both sides of an issue.

   a. Identify a current world issue or problem you would like to discuss.

   b. Write a Yes/No question that suggests an action to be taken on this issue. For example, "Should scientists try to stop global warming?"

   c. Half of the group thinks of reasons to support a "yes" answer to your question. Half of the group thinks of reasons to support a "no" answer.

   d. After discussing the issue, reach a conclusion as a group and report it to the class.

3. Write your own persuasive essay on one of the issues discussed in class. Write at least three paragraphs, including as many details and examples as you can. Try to convince your readers to agree with your point of view.

Crossword Puzzle

Use words from the reading to complete the crossword puzzle.

Across:

2 *War of the* _____

4 Prank

8 Weak; feeble

9 Visitors from outer space

10 Central character in a drama

11 Scientist who studies the stars

14 You can do it with a cup of coffee

16 Describes a sequence of events

17 Not professional

Down:

1 Ancient Greek philosopher

3 Very small life forms

5 Unidentified flying _____

6 One who observes something

7 Hallmarks

9 Type of evidence based on personal stories

10 Experts in the field

12 A type of telescope

13 A very long period of time

15 FUDD: follow up detection _____

Carl Ally   A well-known figure in the field of advertising, Carl Ally (1924–1999) started as a copywriter in New York, where he met art director Amil Gargano. The two partners started their own advertising agency in 1962, which quickly became wildly successful because of Ally's brash and innovative style. Ally also inspired many others to think of doing old things in new and original ways.

Johann Gutenberg   The inventor of the printing press was born in the last part of the fourteenth century in Mainz, Germany. Having developed his skill as a metalworker, Gutenberg spent most of his life in Germany and Strasbourg, France, as a craftsman and inventor. After inventing the printing press, he spent many years trying to perfect his creation and fell into debt as a result. Eventually, he lost his invention to his creditors and ended up living most of his life operating a small printing shop. He was largely unable to take credit for the famous works produced on the new printing machine, and therefore it is difficult for historians to point to who is responsible for some famous copies of the Bible. Gutenberg died on February 3, 1468.

movable type   This was an essential part of Gutenberg's invention. To make movable type, he created a metal mold of each letter of the alphabet in capital and lower case form. Then he collected the letters that he needed into a frame. By doing this, he was able to press out copies at an unprecedented rate. Before Gutenberg's invention, books were copied by hand or printed using carved wood blocks. These methods were extremely slow compared to Gutenberg's new invention that could press out approximately 300 copies each day.

Grace Hopper   A pioneer in the field of computer science, Grace Murray Hopper (1906–1992), was also an officer in the United States Navy and a research mathematician. Her most famous invention was the compiler, a program that translates instructions from English into computer language. This and many other contributions paved the way for later developments that make today's high-speed digital computing possible.

Franz Joseph Haydn   Born near Vienna, Austria, in 1732, Franz Joseph Haydn became one of the most important and influential composers of his time. He wrote over 80 string quartets, at least 104 symphonies, and a number of cantatas and oratorios. Among his most famous works are the "Surprise" and "London" symphonies.

duke   A powerful local leader in European history, usually a member of the ruling family, and second in power to a prince. The title still exists in England for several members of the royal family. The wife of a duke is called a *duchess*, and their children are addressed as *lords* and *ladies*.

Pablo Picasso   Regarded by many as the most important European artist of the twentieth century, Picasso is known around the world for his imaginative paintings, drawings, and sculptures. Picasso was born in Spain in 1881 and moved to Paris in 1900, where he began experimenting with different styles of painting. His first original style has been called the Blue Period, after which he developed many other original ways of depicting life through art. He lived in France and continued producing masterpieces until his death in 1973.

Nobel Prize   This is a prestigious award that is presented each year to individuals to honor their groundbreaking work and innovation in the fields of literature, medicine, physics, chemistry, economics, and international peace. The tradition of the Nobel Prize that began in 1901 was created in the will of the Swedish inventor Albert Nobel who wanted his assets and estate to be used to finance these prizes. Various committees in Norway and Sweden choose the annual winners and award them the Nobel Prize for their work that helps the "good of humanity" (Alfred Nobel).

Albert Szent-Györgyi   Born in Budapest, Hungary, in 1893, Dr. Szent-Györgyi is best known for the discovery of actin, a muscle protein. His research also explained the role of vitamins in metabolism and the structure of muscle tissue. He received the Nobel Prize for medicine in 1937.

court fool   In the sixteenth and seventeenth centuries, the court fool was a person appointed by a ruler to entertain members of the royal families and their guests. A court fool, also known as a jester, often dressed in a coat of many colors and wore long, pointed shoes. Court fools specialized in telling jokes and riddles to keep their audiences amused.

yuppie   This stands for *Young Urban Professional*. The term, which was first used in the 1980s, refers to a successful young professional person who lives in or near a large city, earns a lot of money, and spends it on expensive things. This is often used in a critical way.

yen   The *yen* in the basic monetary unit of Japan. Coins worth 5, 10, 50, 100, and 500 yen are used, and paper money is printed in denominations of 1000, 5000, and 10000.

labor union   The main purpose of a labor union is to improve the lives of its members; however, the methods used to achieve this goal vary widely from country to country. A labor union begins by organizing workers into a group and establishing a leadership that meets with the employer to bargain for better pay and benefits.

Japanese education system   In Japan, public school education is free for children from 6 to 14 years old. Public school students attend classes five and a half days per week, and during the last two years of junior high school, often focus on gaining admission to a good high school. Admission to the most prestigious high schools is very competitive, and many students spend several hours a day at private academies preparing to take entrance exams. Their hope is that once they gain entry to an elite high school, they will be assured of getting into one of the country's top universities.

Dr. Frankenstein   The main character in the novel, *Frankenstein*, written by Mary Shelley in 1818. In the story, Dr. Frankenstein is a scientist who creates a living being by putting together parts of dead bodies. At first, the creature is gentle and intelligent, but is rejected and feared because of his horrible appearance. The loneliness resulting from this rejection eventually turns him into a terrible, murderous monster. Many horror movies have been based on the story of Dr. Frankenstein, and the story is sometimes used as a warning against the dangers involved in scientific experimentation with life.

apothecaries   *Apothecary* is an old, rarely used term for today's pharmacist, druggist, or chemist (in British English). Some establishments that sell medicines still use the term, "apothecary shop." Before the days of modern medical practice, apothecaries played a very important role in the diagnosis of disease and the preparation of medicines. Medieval apothecaries mixed their remedies from a selection of their own herbs and potions, and often added magical sayings to increase the potency of their cures.

Hindu surgeons   The practice of medicine in ancient India was based in Hindu religious traditions, and included highly developed surgical techniques. Operations performed by Hindu surgeons included the removal of kidney stones and the removal of cataracts to improve vision. They were also the first known practitioners of plastic surgery, especially the reconstruction of noses.

Food and Drug Administration   An agency of the U.S. government that regulates the preparation and sale of foods and medicines. For example, any prescription medicine sold in the United States must first be approved by the FDA.

take one's shirt off in public   In American teenage culture, many boys enjoy taking off their shirts during the warmer months of the year when they are playing outdoors. This gives them the opportunity to enjoy the sunshine and show off their muscles to their friends.

pitcher   In the game of baseball, the pitcher is the player who throws the ball in the direction of home plate, where a hitter uses a bat to try and hit the ball as far as possible. The pitcher tries to throw the ball so fast that the batter cannot hit it easily or well. A good pitcher must have a very strong arm and quick reflexes.

line drive   A line drive is a type of hit in which the baseball leaves the bat very fast at an angle that is parallel to the ground. Line drives are difficult to catch because they are hit so hard. When baseball players are injured, it is often because they have been hit by a line drive.

BMX bike racing   The short name for *bicycle motocross*—an exciting individual sport that has gained popularity in recent years. BMX riders use specially equipped bicycles to compete in races on rugged outdoor courses. The courses usually have steep hills and difficult turns that make the races tough and dangerous.

World Cup The World Cup, one of the most famous international competitions, is held every four years. All-star teams from 32 nations compete in this tournament for the world championship in soccer. World Cup 2002, which was co-hosted by South Korea and Japan, was the first time the tournament was held in Asia.

real The *real* (pronounced /re'ɑl/) is the basic unit of currency in Brazil. Since the late 1990s, the real has been devalued several times in an effort to attract more foreign investment. However, this has caused the real to have an unstable exchange rate, which in turn has made it difficult for Brazil to pay its foreign debts.

carnival The Brazilian Carnival is a huge, noisy street party in Rio de Janeiro that lasts for four days every February or March. In Latin American countries, any joyful outdoor celebration, especially one with colorful costumes, dancing, and loud music is known as a carnival. In North America, a carnival may have games and mechanical rides to amuse both children and adults.

soccer Also known in many countries as *football*, soccer is the world's most popular sport. The word *soccer* comes from an abbreviation of the game's full name, assoc. (association) football. The game was first played in England in the 1800s, and is now enjoyed by millions of people all over the world.

FIFA *Fédération Internationale de Football Association* is the international governing body that establishes the rules for professional soccer throughout the world and organizes international competitions. FIFA consists of the national soccer associations of more than 150 countries, and is based in Zurich, Switzerland.

Olympics The Olympic Games began in ancient Greece in 776 B.C., and continued until A.D. 393. The modern games, which were first held in 1896, have become the most important international athletic competition in the world. The Olympics are held in a different host country every four years for the purpose of promoting friendship and sporting competition for the youth of the world. The Olympics are organized by the International Olympic Committee (IOC), which has its headquarters in Lousanne, Switzerland. The IOC approves the sports to be included in the games, and also selects the host city for the next Olympics seven years in advance.

"Dave, ..."   It is common in workplace environments in the United States for employees to address their supervisors informally and directly, using their first names.

a caring and understanding environment   This phrase reflects a management style which seeks to create a relaxed atmosphere in the workplace. According to this type of thinking, employees who feel free to express their ideas and feelings will be more productive and loyal.

emotionally charged words   There are several levels of such words, depending on the level of emotion that the speaker feels. For example, in the opening conversation between Bill and Dave, Bill tells Dave that he's "never around anymore." While this is a criticism, the level of emotion expressed in the words is relatively low. The words indicate that Bill is upset, but he is in control of his anger. If Bill were angrier, he might say, "Everybody knows you're lazy."

variety of slang   Slang is a form of very informal, sometimes playful language that is used among family, friends, and often among co-workers. The type of slang people in the United States use depends on many factors, including the region they live in, ethnic group, social status, and age. The meaning of a slang term may easily change with time, or may have different meanings within different groups.

nonverbal behavior   Patterns of communicating nonverbally vary considerably from culture to culture. For example, in most Western cultures, looking at a person directly is considered a positive behavior when listening or speaking, whereas in many Eastern cultures, it is considered disrespectful or even rude. In some cultures a friendly facial expression and pleasant tone of voice may be considered inappropriate for a supervisor because it signals lack of proper manners for a person in that position.

Nebraska   A state with a population of approximately 1.5 million people located in the central region of the United States.

TV Western   Television show about life in the western region of the United States, sometimes known as the "Wild West." These stories are usually set in the nineteenth century, and many tell the stories of brave cowboys and pioneers as they face the challenges of settling in a wild and dangerous land. Other stories portray the conflict between unruly outlaws and the heroic defenders of law and order.

William James (1842–1910)   William James was an important American philosopher and psychologist. He is considered one of the major thinkers in a philosophical movement known as pragmatism, which contends that the meaning of any idea lies in its practical results. In his major work, *Principles of Psychology* (1890), James explored the relationship among experience, thought, and action.

Walter Lippmann (1889–1974)   Walter Lippmann was a well-known journalist and philosopher originally from New York City. After graduating from Harvard University in 1910 and working in several government positions, Lippmann began his career as a reporter and columnist. Several U.S. presidents asked him for advice, and in 1918, he helped President Woodrow Wilson draft his famous peace proposal known as The Fourteen Points. In his writings, Lippmann expressed the view that civilized societies must be governed by reason rather than emotion and economic self-interest.

S.I. Hayakawa (1906–1992)   Samuel Ichiye Hayakawa was born in the Canadian province of British Columbia and studied English Literature at McGill University in Montreal. Soon after receiving his Ph.D. from the University of Wisconsin, Hayakawa wrote *Language in Action*, which became a best-selling college textbook in the field of semantics. In 1955, Dr. Hayakawa accepted a teaching position at San Francisco State College in California, where he later became acting president and became involved in politics. At the age of 70, Dr. Hayakawa was elected to the United States Senate, where he became well known for his conservative views.

a few good men   This expression refers to the personal qualities of honesty and strict ethical behavior. In 1992, the term's popularity became more widespread because it was used as the title of a movie about the U.S. Marine Corps (*A Few Good Men*, starring Tom Cruise, Jack Nicholson, and Demi Moore). The film presents the American military as a system without a strong moral code and depicts how a few ethical people work to rid the system of corruption.

cyberrelationships   This term refers to a new phase of human interactions that has become possible with the widespread use of computer technology. Through venues such as dating services, role-playing games, and chat rooms, people meet online and usually connect based on common interest or intent. The development of this kind of relationship is different from traditional courting practices, since people get to know each other well long before they meet face to face.

the Internet   Formally known as the International Computer Network, the Internet is the foundation of a communication technology. The system links thousands of individual networks such as government agencies, educational systems, and commercial and industrial groups. These links allow people to access posted information from each of the participating groups. Some popular features of the Internet include e-mail, e-commerce, e-learning, chat rooms, and the Web.

the Web   The World Wide Web is a feature of the Internet. This feature works as a library in that it organizes information into a format that is easy to use and understand online. Web users can access the text, files, or services they want through a focused search. The Web applies a technology (Hypertext Technology) that makes it accessible to people of many different backgrounds.

match-maker   In many cultures, this term has traditionally meant someone who arranges marriages. Often this union is made for political or economic reasons as demonstrated in history by the royal courts of Europe, and the social structures of India and China. Matchmaking in the United States may be done informally by a mutual friend or, more formally, by a dating agency that pairs people based on their personalities and interests.

former U.S.S.R.   Before its breakup in 1991, the Union of Soviet Socialist Republics (U.S.S.R.), also known as the Soviet Union, covered more than half of Europe and nearly two-fifths of Asia. The former republics include Russia, Latvia, Belarus, and Kyrgyztan. At its height, the U.S.S.R. was an industrial giant and a leader in space exploration. The Soviet Union was considered one of two ranking superpowers, and its rivalry with the United States defined much of the history of the world between 1940 and 1990.

e-mail order brides   Before e-mail, there were systems for mail-order brides in areas where women were scarce. This gave communities a greater chance of survival. Europeans in Australia and the Americas participated in this system when they were spreading out onto these continents. The current trend of e-mail order brides continues the tradition in many ways. The couple have not met each other except through written communication, and the husband-to-be is most likely the source of money. However, the reasons for this kind of union today are different from those in history. Women are not in limited numbers, but as technology brings different countries into closer contact, one may consider the cultural advantages of a partner from another country.

mafia   The mafia, also referred to as "the mob," has had quite a famous history in the United States from the earliest part of the twentieth century with the peak of the industrial period. The mafia creates a structure where crime is not committed by one person, but by a group of people working in a defined system of illegal activity such as the drug trade. The mafia's hired men have leaders that are responsible for all the activity and very difficult to arrest because they never actually take part in any crime. Organized crime exists in many ethnic groups such as the Russian Mafia and Chinese Mafia.

September 11   September 11th marks the tragic day in 2001 when hijackers flew two commercial airliners into the World Trade Towers in New York City and a third into the Pentagon (U.S. military headquarters) in Washington, D.C. The twin towers in New York were completely destroyed, and the Pentagon was seriously damaged. A fourth hijacked airplane crashed into the ground before reaching its target. In all, over 3,000 people were killed, including all of the passengers and crew aboard the airliners.

supply and demand   In the field of economics, this term is used to describe how well a product sells. Manufacturers watch for changes in the requests for their product and modify their production accordingly. If sales are not going well, they change their product or decrease production in order to create demand.

Dairy Queen   A fast-food chain based in Minneapolis, Minnesota, Dairy Queen drive-in restaurants feature soft-serve ice cream, milk shakes, and other desserts. Founded in 1940 as a small store selling ice cream, the menu now includes hamburgers, sandwiches, salads, and drinks. There are nearly 6,000 restaurants in the U.S., Canada, and in 20 other countries around the world.

Concordia College   Concordia is a private liberal arts and sciences college located in Moorhead, Minnesota. The college, which has approximately 3,000 students, emphasizes Christian values and community service.

Ms. Lee-Cadwell   Since the rise of the feminist movement in the 1970s, it has become more common for American women to keep their family name after they marry. Some do not change their name at all, while others hyphenate their own last name with their husbands'.

registered dietitian   In order to become a registered dietitian (RD) in the United States, a person must complete a bachelor's degree and pass a national examination.

University of Southern California   USC is a large, private research university located in Los Angeles, California. In addition to 17 professional schools, USC has one of the country's largest and respected teaching hospitals.

kimchi   Pickled cabbage (or other vegetables) prepared according to ancient methods developed in Korea starting around the seventh century. Kimchi is processed with a mixture of red pepper powder, garlic, ginger, green onion, and radish. Kimchi has become popular in Western countries as an appetizer or addition to a main course.

University of North Carolina   UNC is the state's public university and offers undergraduategraduate and graduate degrees in over 100 fields including liberal arts, sciences, and medicine. The main campus is located in Chapel Hill.

Tufts University   As one of the leading private universities in the United States, Tufts has a reputation for academic excellence in several fields, including liberal arts, international relations, engineering, and veterinary science. Tufts is located in Medford, Massachusetts (a suburb of Boston), and has a student body of 8,500.

Michigan State University   MSU is a public university in Michigan and was first in the country to teach scientific agriculture. Today, MSU has a student body of approximately 45,000.

Meredith College   Meredith College is a private four-year college for women located in Raleigh, North Carolina. Founded in 1891, Meredith College has a student body of approximately 2,400 students and offers degrees in a range of academic and career-oriented subjects, including a Master's Degree in Nutrition.

William Paterson University   This private university in Paterson, New Jersey, was named after William Paterson (1745–1806), a respected statesman and patriot. The university began as a teacher-training college, but today offers degrees in a wide variety of fields and has 11,000 students.

Centers for Disease Control and Prevention   The CDC is an agency of the U.S. Department of Health and Services. Its mission is to promote health by preventing and controlling disease, injury, and disability. Among its many activities, the CDC provides information regarding health and disease prevention to the public free of charge.

Lewis Carroll   This is the name used by Charles Lutwidge Dodgson (1832–1898), when he published his stories about a young girl named Alice and her travels in a magical world called Wonderland. Although he was a mathematician and a don, or professor, at Oxford University in Britain, and wrote math textbooks, he is best known for the books *Alice's Adventures in Wonderland* (1865) and *Through the Looking Glass* (1872).

Sega   Sega Corporation is a leading international video game company based in Tokyo, Japan. Online games developed by Sega include "Fantasy Star Online" and "Super Monkey Ball."

"The Sims"   The game title is derived from *simulated* and is used in hundreds of other game titles such as "Space Sims," "Combat Sims," and "Flight Sims." In all of these games, the player participates in creating real-life characters and situations.

extended family   This term refers to a person's entire family, including grandparents, in-laws, and cousins. In much of the industrialized world, extended families rarely live together in the same physical location; instead, the great majority of people live in small, nuclear families consisting only of parents and their children.

Amelia Earhart   Amelia Earhart (1898–1937) was a famous American aviator and the first woman to fly solo across the Atlantic Ocean.

Esperanto   Esperanto is an international language invented by Polish doctor Ludwik L. Zamenhof, in the late nineteenth century in the hope that it would help peoples of the world communicate better through a common language. Esperanto has a simple, uniform structure and a vocabulary similar to that of many Western European languages.

"curiouser and curiouser"   Throughout her adventures in Wonderland, the fictional character, Alice, often repeats this phrase to herself to express her amazement about the strange world she is visiting. For those familiar with the character, it has become a way of expressing wonder or dismay at anything that seems odd or unexpected.

Broadway The street in New York City that became famous for its theater during the first decades of the twentieth century. Broadway, also known as "The Great White Way" because of the bright lights lining the street, is a renowned and respected place for professional actors to gain recognition and fame for their skills.

Laurence Fishburne (1961–) Widely acclaimed African American actor and director. Fishburne has starred in a number of major Hollywood movies, including *Apocalypse Now*, *Othello*, *What's Love Got to Do With It?*, and *The Matrix*.

organized consumer movement In an organized consumer movement, buyers respond to the ways a product is produced or how it affects their lives, and companies change their manufacturing processes to address new needs. For example, some people dislike the idea that shampoos or soaps are tested on animals because they believe it is cruel. In response to this, many companies changed the way their products were tested and advertise the fact that they are not tested on animals.

University of Toronto Located in Toronto, Ontario, the University of Toronto is Canada's largest university. With a student body of more than 55,000 graduate and undergraduate students, the U of T is also the country's leading research university.

Fordham University A large, private university in New York City operated by the Roman Catholic Church. Known for its high academic standards, Fordham grants degrees in liberal arts and sciences as well as in business administration. Among its graduate schools is the internationally acclaimed Fordham School of Law.

Information Millennium Also known as the "Information Age," this phrase refers to a new era in the history of the world in which technology has become focused on high-speed communication and access to information. We see this particularly with the widespread use of the Internet and cell phones. People can use these technologies to conduct business faster and more efficiently. Such devices that save time, also work to place an emphasis on a more fast-paced, work-oriented lifestyle.

power brokers and beautiful people   This phrase refers to the reputation of New York City as a bustling center for rich, powerful, and famous people. Much of what separates this group of people as elite is their emphasis on current fashion and posh social life.

Emily Post   Emily Post (1873–1960) was the author of *Etiquette: A Guide to Proper Social Behavior*, published in 1922. She also wrote a newspaper column that advised people on good social manners and taste. Today there are many advice columns that answer people's questions on conduct in difficult situations.

National Highway Traffic Safety Administration   An agency of the U.S. Federal Government that regulates and promotes safety on the nation's roads.

a man who does no reading   Until the emergence of the feminist movement, it was common for writers to refer to all humans as "a man" or "mankind." In recent years, this usage is viewed as outmoded and sexist because it excludes women. Today, a more acceptable way to express the same idea would be to use "a person" in place of "a man" or "humankind" in place of "mankind."

Mencius   This is one of the names of the famous Chinese philosopher whose ideas contributed to the philosophy known as Confucianism. His real name was Meng Ke, and Mencius is the Latin form of Menzi, a Chinese title that means "Master Meng." Mencius was born in the state of Zou, in what is now Shandong Province, in the fourth century B.C. and lived for approximately 80 years. He is best known for his teachings that human nature is essentially good, and that people are justified in overthrowing a ruler who ignores their welfare.

Ssuma Ch'ien (Sima Qian)   In the tradition of Confucius, Sima Qian (145–85 B.C.) demonstrated a deep respect for learning and believed that the rulers of ancient China were chosen by heaven. After extensive travels, he was appointed grand historian in the court of the emperor Han Wudi and proceeded to write the first comprehensive history of China.*

Sung poets   Poets who lived and wrote during the Sung (or Song) dynasty (960–1279 A.D.). Poets of this period were reknowned for *ci*, a popular form of poetry that is often performed with music.

Su Tungp'o (Su Dong-po)   Another name for Su Shi, an important poet of the Song period. His most famous poem, "Song by the River," is still popular today and is still recited or sung during the Mid-Autumn festival.

Sophocles   One of the great dramatists of ancient Greece, Sophocles (about 496–406 B.C.) wrote plays about the struggle of strong individuals against fate. Most of his dramas are tragedies in which the main characters (heroes) suffer from this struggle or die, but through their suffering become more heroic. Sophocles was almost 90 years old when he wrote his greatest tragedy, *Oedipus at Colonus*.

---

* The translator of this text used spellings that are different from those that are commonly used today. Correct spellings are given in parentheses.

Five-foot shelf of Dr. Eliot A well-respected, comprehensive list of books compiled by Harvard president Charles W. Eliot (1834–1926). The five-foot shelf consists of 50 volumes of classic literature which Dr. Eliot believed everyone should read in order to become educated.

Hamlet One of English literature's most famous tragedies by William Shakespeare (1564–1616). The play is best known for its eloquent language, especially for Prince Hamlet's famous speech on suicide, which begins "To be, or not to be…."

G.K. Chesterton A popular English author who lived in London from 1874 to 1936, Chesterton is best known for his mystery stories, biographies, and essays.

George Eliot This was the pen name of Many Ann Evans, an English writer who lived from 1819 to 1880. She is best known for her novels about English country people, in which she touches on themes of moral and social responsibility. Her works include *Silas Marner* and *Middlemarch: A Study of Provincial Life.*

Rousseau Jean-Jacques Rousseau (1712–1778) was a French philosopher whose radical ideas helped shape the political events that eventually lead to the French Revolution. In his writing, Rousseau attacked the existing structure by charging that private property was the cause of inequality and oppression. In addition to his philosophical essays, Rousseau wrote novels, poetry, and a full-length opera.

Nietzsche Friedrich Nietzsche (1844–1900) was a German philosopher who is best known for his criticism of traditional religious beliefs and values. Nietzsche's ideal was to be able to control one's emotions and use them in a creative manner. His major works were *Thus Spake Zarathustra* and *Beyond Good and Evil.*

Schopenhauer The German philosopher Arthur Schopenhauer (1788–1860) became famous toward the end of his life for his ideas on how people experience the world. His theories about true inner nature of human beings led to his suggestion that happiness can best be achieved through the contemplation of beauty.

SETI (search for extraterrestrial intelligence) This term most often refers to a private, nonprofit organization of scientists and educators known as the SETI Institute. Founded in 1984, SETI Institute is dedicated to exploring and explaining the origin and existence of life in the universe.

Hollywood Hollywood, California, is a district of the city of Los Angeles with a population of approximately 280,000. Because of its mild climate and variety of natural scenery, Hollywood became a center for the film industry, and today it is known as the motion-picture capital of the world.

UFOs (unidentified flying objects) UFOs are unusual lights or objects people believe they see flying in the air. Although many people report having seen alien spacecraft, investigators usually have discovered ordinary explanations. For example, meteors that hit the earth's atmosphere can cause unusual light effects. However, a small number of UFO sightings have not been explained, and many people around the world continue to believe that the earth has already been visited by creatures from outer space.

Orson Welles (1915–1985) Orson Welles was a celebrated American actor and director. While still in his twenties, he acted in numerous radio plays and later became a prominent film actor. He was best known for his performance in the film, *Citizen Kane*, which he also co-wrote and directed. Many critics regard it as the best movie ever made.

The War of the Worlds The title of a novel about an invasion from Mars written in 1898 by British author H.G. Wells. In 1938, the novel was made into a realistic radio play starring Orson Welles. The broadcast caused widespread public panic by convincing many listeners that martians were actually invading New Jersey (U.S.A.).

NASA (National Aeronautics and Space Administration) NASA is a large agency of the U.S. government which coordinates scientific research on space flight. NASA projects have included *Apollo 11* in 1969, which was the first spacecraft to land human beings on the moon, as well as the *Columbia* and *Discovery* space shuttles. NASA has also sent unmanned probes to Mars and has begun work with other nations on the construction of an International Space Station.

Arecibo dish   The huge metal reflector of the world's largest radio telescope, located in Puerto Rico. The dish is fitted with a transmitter that is able to send radio signals into deep space.

Very Large Array (VLA)   A system of 27 movable radio telescopes built on railroad tracks in the shape of a Y, located in New Mexico. The movements of the telescope are coordinated by astronomers seeking to detect and identify the radio waves sent out by celestial objects.

New Mexico   A state in the southwestern United States on the border of Mexico, with a population of over 1,500,000 people. New Mexico has been home to much scientific research, including astronomy, for many years.

Contact   The title of a popular science-fiction movie (1985) based on the novel by Carl Sagan. In the film, a brilliant young scientist, Dr. Ellie Arroway (played by Jodie Foster), receives a radio message from the distant star, Vega. The countries of the world work together to decode the aliens' message, and Ellie volunteers to be the person to make first contact with them. The movie differs from many other Hollywood versions of aliens in that they are depicted as intelligent beings with good intentions toward less-advanced civilizations.

Aristotle (384–322 B.C.)   Aristotle was a Greek philosopher and scientist who is considered to have had one of the greatest influences on Western culture. Among Aristotle's writings are the *Organon*, which investigates the nature of thought, and *Physics*, the study of things that change. As a scientist, he collected an enormous amount of information about the variety and structure of animals and plants. He was also interested in the movement of the stars and planets, and recorded his observations in a book called *On the Heavens*.

Map 1 **Europe and the Former U.S.S.R.**

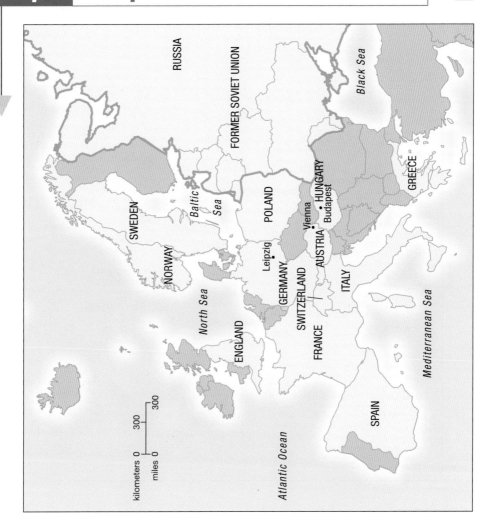

Map 2 | Asia

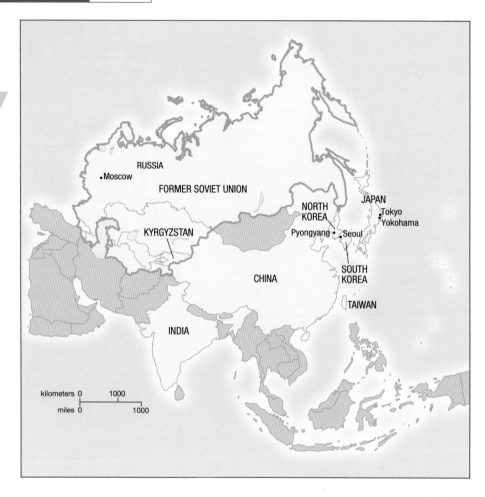

RUSSIA
•Moscow
FORMER SOVIET UNION
NORTH
KOREA
JAPAN
•Tokyo
•Yokohama
KYRGYZSTAN
Pyongyang • •Seoul
CHINA
SOUTH
KOREA
TAIWAN
INDIA

kilometers 0   1000
miles 0   1000

Map 3 **North America**

British
Columbia

Ontario

MN

WI

Milwaukee

Toronto

NY

Boston

MA

Ithaca

Long Island

Pacific
Ocean

NE

Chicago

MI

Cleveland

NJ

New York

OH

CA

IL

Washington,
D.C.

MD

St. Louis

MO

Atlantic
Ocean

Los Angeles

NM

NC

kilometers 0   300

miles 0   300

FL

Gulf of
Mexico

Puerto
Rico

Map 4 | South America

Caribbean Sea

Atlantic
Ocean

Pacific
Ocean

BRAZIL

ARGENTINA

kilometers 0   500

miles 0   500

Map 5 **Africa**

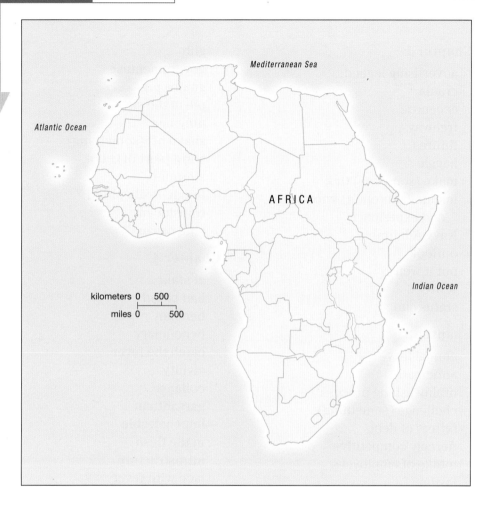

Mediterranean Sea

Atlantic Ocean

AFRICA

Indian Ocean

kilometers 0   500
miles 0   500

Vocabulary Index

Chapter 5

bounce ideas off of (someone)
build rapport
clarifying question
emotionally charged word
fake attention
feel swamped
flight-or-fight mode
grill
listen empathetically
(one's) never around
nonjudgmentally
nonverbal cue
personal bias
put down
semantic barrier
slang
tend to assume
the way things are going
zero in on

Chapter 6

big, recognizable cut-out
blind-date
chastening thought
country yokel
delve into the main asset
din into (someone)
for all the fact that
grade B movie
horn-rimmed glasses
inimitable
perfectly synchronized
quite literally
racketeer
reactionary
start from scratch
swarthy
telephone stock swindler
testimony
topple a whole edifice of ideas
warp

Chapter 7

bachelorette

baneful social indicator
bio
burned
dabble in (something)
false identity
fatalistic
go on record
go sour
gushing
hit (someone) up for cash
market
match made in heaven
mundane
paradoxically
pique (someone's) interest
potential suitor
predator
put a damper on (something)
ripped off
string (someone) along
thug
workaholic
would-be bride

Chapter 8

bang my head against a wall
binge and purge
calorie
carbonated beverage
chicken tenders
compulsive overeating and
    undereating
condiment
dreaded freshman 15
eating disorder
ethnic
go to greater lengths
kiosk
mandatory
obesity
obsession
predecessor
sloppy joe
talk the talk, but don't walk the
    walk